New England's Best Family Getaways

By Dan and Roberta LaPlante

COVERED BRIDGE PRESS
NORTH ATTLEBOROUGH, MA

Publisher's Cataloging in Publication

LaPlante, Daniel James, 1956-
New England's Best Family Getaways/Dan and Roberta LaPlante.
p. cm.
Includes index.
ISBN 0-924771-73-9
1. Bed and breakfast accommodations–New England–Guide-books. 2. New England–Description and travel–1981–Guide books. I. LaPlante, Roberta Sullivan, 1961-II. Title.

TX907.3.A35L3 1992   647.947403
                                      QBI92-566

Library of Congress Catalog Card Number: 94-069865

Cover Design by Don Langevin
Illustrated by Constance Mayfield

Second Printing

To Ryan, Peter, and Laura

New England

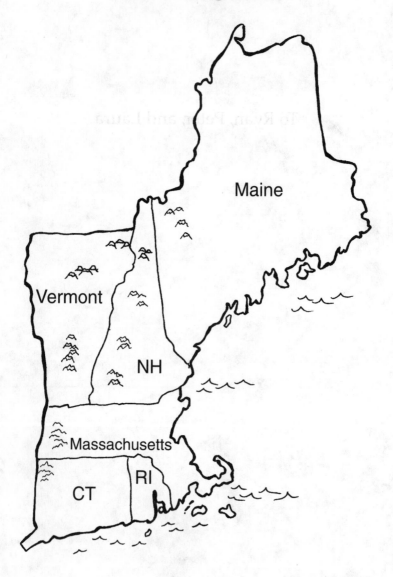

Table of Contents

Introduction

This is a book for families who enjoy traveling. Whether as an overnight stop on the way to Grandma's or as a vacation destination, the establishments profiled in this guidebook offer comfortable and often unique accommodations for families. Country inns and B&B's have become a very popular alternative to other types of lodging in recent years. Honeymooners, vacationing couples, retirees, naturalists, and history buffs have become regular visitors to the expanding number of inns and B&B's that have been established across the length and breadth of New England. This guidebook allows families as well to enlist themselves as the newest group of B&B and country inn enthusiasts.

Children can cause some complications for families desiring the unique type of experience that country inns provide. Many inns and B&B's specialize in a type of hospitality more appropriate for adults. Traveling families are justifiably concerned about how comfortable they will feel in a country inn. Is the place furnished with priceless antiques? Is it all right if the baby makes a mess of her breakfast? Can adjoining rooms be arranged? Is a little bit of typical family noise acceptable? These questions and more have been asked of every innkeeper we have met. We have kept family needs foremost in our minds when we interviewed the hundreds of candidates for inclusion in this guide.

You will find a rich variety of country inns and B&B's in this book. In New Hampshire, you might get lost for a week at a working farm complete with early morning chores and country style cooking. Breakfast can be delivered to your private cottage in coastal Maine. Travel back to Colonial times at a B&B in Connecticut where open hearth cooking and period costumes are featured. From the majestic Green Mountains in Vermont to the sandy beaches of Cape Cod, the establishments featured herein provide unique getaways which meet the needs of all types of families. Whether you are traveling with a tot or seeking adventure with teenagers, you will surely be able to find a special place to build your family memories.

We have drawn a distinction between establishments that "accept children" and those that truly welcome families. Only inns and B&B's where families will feel comfortable are included in this guide. Sometimes the warmth and charisma of the innkeeper was particularly attractive. Or perhaps another B&B has accommodations that are especially appropriate for children. Regardless of the unique characteristics of all the wonderful places included in this guide, they all share the common thread of family-friendliness. New England offers an endless variety of family activities. The country inns and B&B's featured herein can be your gateway to many regional splendors.

Hundreds of inns and B&B's were considered for this book. We have recommended only the most appropriate family destinations. Each country inn and B&B has been personally visited by our family. They have been child tested by our own children. We have spent time with each innkeeper and have made independent assessments of their attitude toward families and their tolerance for children. We have been taken with the wonderful perspectives and warm, caring qualities that innkeepers possess. It seems that some of the most pleasant and interesting people end up as proprietors of country inns and B&B's.

No fees have been charged to innkeepers for inclusion in this book. No innkeepers association or industry group has sponsored our effort in any way. As a result, we have been able to make our own selections based entirely on our experiences as guests at each establishment featured in this book. Users of this guide can take comfort in the fact that they are reading completely independent reviews.

There are some rules of the road that are helpful for traveling families to keep in mind. First of all, nobody knows their inn or B&B better than the innkeeper. When you make a reservation, please be specific about your particular family requirements. Based on the size and age of your family, the length of your stay, and other factors, the innkeeper will usually suggest the most appropriate accommodations. Please allow them this function. The innkeepers usually have very good ideas in this regard, and if a larger room or private entrance is suggested, it is always well worth the nominal expense. Parents need to be responsible for their children. Although each establishment included in this guide is a wonderful place for a family, consideration for other guests is always necessary. If a child is upset or disruptive, it is important for parents to deal promptly with the situation in order to maintain proper public harmony. If your child is not doing well at the breakfast table or is having trouble sleeping, most innkeepers can offer some very helpful alternatives. Please feel free to ask them for help.

The selection process we used to produce this collection of inns and B&B's has been exhaustive and has focused on family needs and interests. We also admit a certain bias in our review toward establishments that are family owned and operated. By and large we have avoided places that felt more like a resort or a hotel than a country inn. Additionally, we were not interested in including B&B's where the owner/innkeeper was not in residence on the property. As a result, you will find the establishments we profile generally fit with a more classic or traditional definition of the country inn and B&B experience. We looked for the personal, friendly service and unique accommodations that have made country inns and B&B's so popular.

Introduction

We are interested in your comments or recommendations. If you have a particularly enjoyable experience, or maybe one that is not very good, feel free to send your thoughts to our publisher. Also, if you know of any great family inn or B&B, let us know so we can consider it for inclusion in future editions. Please send your comments to:

Dan and Roberta LaPlante
c/o Covered Bridge Press
7 Adamsdale Road
N. Attleborough, MA 02760

How To Use This Guide

The inns in this guide are listed in alphabetic order within each state by town and inn name.

Rates:

All rates quoted are for double occupancy, unless otherwise stated. They may vary by season or length of stay. Charges for extra persons, cribs, etc. vary as well. We use several standard abbreviations to indicate what is included in quoted rates as follows:

EP: European plan; no meals included.

B&B: Breakfast included in room rate; varies from light continental to multi-course.

MAP: Modified American plan; rates include breakfast and dinner.

AP: American plan; quoted rates include three meals a day.

Quoted rates are subject to change, so be sure to check with innkeepers when you make a reservation. We have made every effort to insure their accuracy as of 1996. Taxes vary by location and are seldom included in quoted rates. Some inns and B&B's automatically add a gratuity (10-15%) to quoted room rates. Others leave the decision to their guests. Ask your innkeeper if a gratuity will be added to your bill. Otherwise, you might want to tip as appropriate to housekeepers, wait persons, etc.

Reservations:

Reservations are required at all the inns and B&B's included in this book. Most of the establishments included in this guide are popular destinations, so early reservations are a good idea. The accommodations typically required by families may require set up prior to arrival, and innkeepers generally prefer to plan ahead for their guests. Personal hospitality, the hallmark of most country inns and B&B's, often requires advance preparation. Dates of operation and accepted methods of payment are included in the reference key following each establishment's review in this guide. Most inns have specific deposit requirements and refund policies. Your innkeeper will review these with you when reservations are made. We encourage patrons to notify innkeepers if your arrival is delayed for any reason. Oftentimes, innkeepers will stay up to personally greet their late arrivals. Common courtesy dictates that you inform your host of your expected arrival time.

Children:

The inns and B&B's featured in this book welcome families with children. Many offer accommodations, activities, and nearby attractions that suit a family's needs. In addition to discussing these areas in each review, the key at the end of each review includes specific information about the availability of cribs, high chairs, and roll-away beds. This information provides a framework for deciding which inn or B&B is right for you. We also encourage you to ask your innkeeper any questions you might have in this area.

Restrictions:

Most establishments have some restriction on cigarette, cigar, and pipe smoking. Unless otherwise mentioned, please plan to take your smoke outdoors. Some inns allow smoking in common areas but few allow it in guest rooms.

Some inns and B&B's have liquor licenses, others do not. Where no liquor license is held, innkeepers often provide setups or ice service for anyone interested in B.Y.O.B. Inquire with your host for the policy at your chosen destination.

Accommodations for pets vary widely. Some B&B's can refer you to a nearby kennel or provide some other support. Many, however, offer no convenient facility for pets. If your pet is an integral part of your travel plans, advance inquiry and early arrangements are a must.

Connecticut

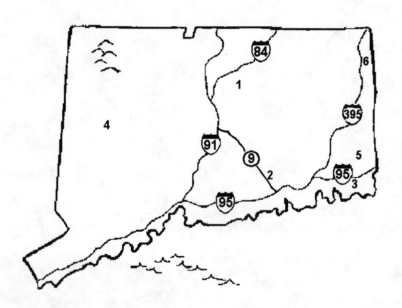

Contents

Jared Cone House

Innkeepers: Jeff and Cinde Smith
Telephone: (203) 643-8538, (203) 649-5678
Address: 25 Hebron Road
*   Bolton, CT 06043*

Innkeepers Jeff and Cinde Smith invite you and your family to enjoy the charm of their historic country home. We took them up on their offer and thoroughly enjoyed our stay at the Jared Cone House. Guests of the Smiths are certain to find an abundance of charm and history in this traditional center-hall Georgian Colonial. The post and beam structure boasts seven fireplaces and a Palladian window above the front door. The house is named after its original owner, a wealthy farmer, and was built in two phases in 1775 and 1800. It also once served as Bolton's library and post office. Their home is now registered with the U.S. Department of the Interior, Office of Archeology and Historic Preservation.

Three spacious bedrooms are available on the second floor with queen size beds, fireplaces, and scenic views of the surrounding countryside. They all will accommodate roll-aways and cribs. One of the rooms has its own bath, and the other two rooms share a bath. The parlor, second floor hallway, and dining room are furnished with antiques and period pieces.

A full country breakfast of homemade breads, fruit, juices, and French toast, eggs, or pancakes is served in the dining room. In the summer you may prefer having breakfast served on the porch. We couldn't help but notice the nanny's rocker in the dining room. It is truly a rare find and at the time Cinde said was not for sale, although she may consider selling other pieces in the B&B.

Towering maples, meticulously groomed lawns, and gardens make up the three acres of property upon which this beautiful home is situated. Behind the barn, children will find a fort. There's also a tree swing that can be seen from the comfort of a wicker rocking chair on the porch.

Jeff and Cinde and their two young children Julie and Drew will make you feel right at home. Jeff's furniture making and restoration business is located in the new post and beam barn behind the house (it's a real beauty).

The Smiths take special pride in the delicious maple syrup they provide for their guests. It is made from their own sugar maple trees and boiled over the massive stone fireplace in the kitchen.

The B&B is just fifteen miles from Hartford and close to many area attractions. If you feel the need to wander from this lovely setting, your hosts have a list of available attractions sure to please the entire family.

Accommodations: 3 guest rooms, 1 room with private bath, 2 rooms with shared bath. Roll-aways and crib available.

Rates: $60-$70, double occupancy, B&B. $10 charge for roll-away bed.

Methods of Payment: Cash, traveler's check, personal check.

Dates of Operation: Open all year.

Children: Appropriate for all ages.

Activities/Facilities: Bicycle riding, and nearby canoeing, antiquing, hiking, and ice skating. Park with playscape, swingset, and basketball court next to the B&B.

The Griswold Inn

Innkeeper: *Sarah Elizabeth Grader*
Telephone: *(203) 767-1776*
Address: *36 Main Street*
Essex, CT 06426

Experience the charm and robust spirit of an authentic Colonial road house at "The Gris." Built in 1776, it has been serving travelers, neighbors, and friends since our country was born. And it is truly authentic. Lots of cozy rooms with low ceilings, exposed beams, and fireplaces are essentially unchanged from their original construction and decor (indoor plumbing and electricity have been added, thankfully). In colonial times, the road house was a gathering place serving many purposes. It was a meeting place for friends, a lodging place for travelers, and a hearty restaurant for all comers. Music, good food, and a warm bed were as welcoming to our ancestors as they are to us today. The Griswold Inn maintains all of these traditions with the benefit of over 220 years of experience.

Owners Bill and Victoria Winterer, who represent only the fifth family to own the inn, are dedicated to preserving the property and the lovely, historic seafaring village of Essex. Innkeeper Sarah Grader is in charge of the staff and oversees the myriad happenings and special events that occur here. You might find anything from banjo players to opera singers performing in the Tap Room each evening.

There are twenty-five guest rooms all including private baths and telephones. A good number of them are suites, with sitting areas ranging from alcove size to full living rooms, and plenty of room to bed most families. The Garden Suite is particularly attractive. It has two double beds and room for a crib or roll-away plus a downstairs sitting area with a fireplace and a wet bar. All guest rooms also include air conditioning and piped-in classical music.

A continental breakfast consisting of fruits, English muffins, cereals, juices, coffee, and tea is served in the library to all overnight guests. But the real culinary attraction is dinner. Plan to dine at the inn at least one evening during your stay. No fewer than six separate dining rooms offer dinner guests a wide range of motifs. The Steamboat Room features nautical artifacts and a steamship mural. We're told that the steamship actually moves up and down if you watch carefully! The Gun Room houses a collection of antique firearms dating to the fifteenth century. The Tap Room has a dark, handsome bar, maritime paintings, and beautiful replica ship models. The menu presents a variety of seafood, fowl, homemade sausage which has been a tradition here since 1776, and a variety of other hearty selections. There is also a young sailors' menu including everything from peanut butter sandwiches to prime rib and bottomless carafes of soda. On Sunday mornings, a special Hunt Breakfast is offered which features a grits-and-cheese souffle, fried chicken, baby cod, broiled kidneys, roasted meats, and enough accompaniments to sate you for the entire day. During

December, a special Christmas dinner menu includes colonial favorites such as venison, pheasant, and rabbit.

While in Essex, you might stroll the narrow village streets, browsing through local shops as you meander toward the waterfront. Or you can visit the River Museum at Steamboat Dock for a recollection of the area's shipbuilding and trading history. A very popular local attraction is the Valley Railroad steam train and river boat ride, which offers a northerly rail journey along the banks of the Connecticut River to a waiting river boat which navigates further up river before returning to the rail head. Essex is a very special place and the Griswold Inn is justifiably its centerpiece.

Accommodations: 25 guest rooms including 11 suites. All rooms have private baths, telephones, air conditioning, and classical music. Cribs and roll-aways available.

Rates: $90-$175, double occupancy, B&B. Additional persons, $10.

Methods of Payment: Cash, traveler's check, personal check, major credit cards.

Dates of Operation: Open all year.

Children: Appropriate for all ages.

Activities/Facilities: Historic accommodations, fine dining, live entertainment. A multitude of shops, cafes, and historic buildings in the immediate area. River excursions, theatres, and state parks nearby.

Red Brook Inn

Innkeeper: Ruth Keyes
Telephone: (203) 572-0349
Address: P.O. Box 237
Old Mystic, CT 06372

If you're looking for a setting that provides a respite from the hectic pace of modern times, look no further than the Red Brook Inn. The inn offers bed and breakfast lodging in two historic buildings; the Haley Tavern, ca. 1740, and the Crary Homestead, ca. 1770. Ruth Keyes, owner and innkeeper as well as antiquarian/history buff, has carefully restored these two eighteenth century Colonials to their original simplicity and elegance. The inn has been personalized by Ruth's artistic stenciling ability, carefully selected period furnishings, handwoven rugs, and coordinating accessories.

The Haley Tavern and Crary Homestead, both authentic center chimney Colonials, feature lovely guest rooms with antique canopy beds and working fireplaces in many of the rooms. Wood is provided and fires laid and lit on chilly evenings. Most of the rooms can accommodate a crib and a few rooms have a double bed and a single. Adjoining rooms can also be provided with advance notice. All rooms have private baths.

Full and hearty country breakfasts are served family style in the Haley Tavern's Keeping Room each morning. Pancakes, waffles, eggs, breakfast meat, fresh fruit, juice, cereal, and coffee are all part of this delightful fare. On cold autumn and winter mornings, guests may enjoy their breakfast before an inviting fire.

Ruth offers special weekend packages in the fall and winter featuring open hearth cooking, a traditional Colonial method of cooking. Roast lamb and turkey are accompanied by homemade bread and pies served hot from the great hearth's brick bake oven.

Over seven secluded acres of wooded countryside surrounded by stone walls are available for exploring. Ruth is a grandmother herself and invites families of all ages to her inn. The Tavern Room houses shelves of books, games, and puzzles. A color TV with cable is also available. A refrigerator to chill a bottle of wine or baby formula can also be found here.

There are many attractions to keep your family on the go while in Mystic and the surrounding area. Most notable would be the Mystic Seaport Museum and Mystic Marinelife Aquarium. Long Island Sound is a short distance from the inn as are antique shops, wineries, and many day trip excursions.

Accommodations: 11 rooms, all with private baths. Crib available.

Rates: $95-$189, double occupancy, B&B. $25 for extra person over 15 years old.

Methods of Payment: Cash, traveler's check, personal check, MasterCard, Visa.

Dates of Operation: Open all year.

Children: Appropriate for all ages.

Activities/Facilities: Weekend packages featuring Colonial cooking in November and December. Nearby historic museums and homes, antique shops, wineries, and various sea port activities.

The Inn on Lake Waramaug

Innkeeper: Nancy Conant
Telephone: (203) 868-0563, (800) LAKE-INN
Address: North Shore Road
New Preston, CT 06777

The Inn on Lake Waramaug welcomes you to the charm and beauty of traditional New England. The inn has been offering hospitality to its guests for nearly 200 years. Its close proximity to New York City makes it a convenient and popular weekend getaway for families and couples alike.

This lovely lakeside inn is situated in the midst of the Litchfield Hills. Activities abound at the inn and in neighboring towns. The inn offers an indoor swimming pool, a game room with pool table, ping-pong, and various board games. A private beach at the lake is also enjoyed by guests who prefer fresh water swimming. You will also find a few canoes and rowboats at the shore's edge. If tennis is your game, a har-tru court is just steps away from the guest rooms. Golf, cross-country and downhill skiing, hiking, and more can all be enjoyed locally. The inn has a reputation for sponsoring many year-round amusing activities which include a frog-jumping jamboree in July, a Huckleberry Finn raft race on Labor Day, a pumpkin carving contest in October, snow sculpturing in January's winter festival, and a maple sugaring festival in March. It would be wise to plan ahead for these popular special events.

Eighteen of the inn's twenty-three guest rooms are located in the Maples and Hawthorne buildings. These rooms have private entrances and most have fireplaces. The main inn has five cozy guest rooms. All rooms have private baths, telephones, and cable television. Each has been uniquely decorated with many having queen size canopy beds and antique furnishings. There is also a small, grassy lawn outside each room where your children can play and still be in earshot.

The accommodations also include a full country breakfast and a dinner menu of inventive American Cuisine. Guests have their choice of a number of entrees which might include roast rack of lamb, grilled yellow fin tuna, honey marinated muscovy duck breast, and other culinary creations. Children's portions are available upon request. You may choose to dine in the inn's lovely dining room or, if you prefer a more casual setting, the patio is available in the summer.

Innkeeper Nancy Conant and her staff are very attentive to their guests' needs. The Inn on Lake Waramaug is sure to become a favorite getaway for you and your family.

Accommodations: 23 rooms, all with private bath. Cribs and roll-aways available.

Rates: $156-$229, double occupancy, MAP. Children's rates available upon request.

Methods of Payment: Cash, traveler's check, personal check, major credit cards.

Dates of Operation: Open all year.

Children: Appropriate for all ages.

Activities/Facilities: Indoor swimming pool, tennis court, game room. Nearby golf, cycling, and skiing.

Randall's Ordinary

Innkeeper: William Foakes
Telephone: (203) 599-4540
Address: P.O. Box 243
North Stonington, CT 06359

Traditional American hearth cooking is what Randall's Ordinary specializes in. Just as the Randalls cooked their meals and delighted their guests by the open hearth 306 years ago, so does the staff at Randall's Ordinary today. The wait staff, authentically dressed in Colonial costume, is very helpful in explaining the menu of poultry, seafood, chops, or roasts. Our meal started off with cornbread and tomato carrot soup. The smoke flavor is subtle and delicious. Roast duck with rhubarb chutney, barbecued pork, and a lamb stew which our children shared were all wonderful. Three dining rooms service the inn for breakfast, lunch, and dinner daily. The inn welcomes the public and group tours for dining.

After dinner, you may retreat to either the second floor of the John Randall house which offers three authentic Colonial rooms, all with fireplaces, or the Jacob Tarpenning barn. This enormous structure, which houses many of the guest rooms, was moved from New York and re-erected over a year's time at Randall's. Various accommodations are particularly attractive for families. They include rooms with queen size canopy beds with double size trundles, and double size four poster beds with sitting lofts reached by spiral staircases. All fifteen rooms have completely modern private baths.

Twenty-seven private acres of New England woods and countryside unfold as you wind yourself through the old-fashioned lampposted drive. Your children will love exploring the grounds, complete with barn, pigs, chickens, oxen in the field, and the simplicity of a tree swing. Randall's is also home to Cricket the burro who loves to be fed apples and carrots. Many area attractions are just minutes away including Mystic Marinelife Aquarium and Rhode Island beaches.

Another attraction at Randall's which your children will enjoy is Ashes, the inn's talking parrot. He's a shy fellow when you first approach, but our kids were able to elicit a good bit of chatter.

Accommodations: 15 rooms, all with private baths.

Rates: $85-$140, double occupancy, B&B. $10 for each additional person in room.

Methods of Payment: Cash, traveler's check, personal check, major credit cards.

Dates of Operation: Open all year.

Children: Appropriate for all ages.

Activities/Facilities: Nearby attractions include beaches, museums, antiquing. Full service inn featuring breakfast, lunch, dinner, and taproom.

Hickory Ridge Bed & Breakfast

Innkeepers: Birdie and Ken Olson
Telephone: (203) 928-9530
Address: 1084 Quaddick Town Farm Road
*   Thompson, CT 06277*

Hickory Ridge Bed & Breakfast offers travelers a chance to enjoy a quiet, beautiful country setting in an area of Connecticut that is still largely rural and steeped in history. The town of Thompson is located in the northeast quadrant of the state, known as Connecticut's "Quiet Corner." The surrounding countryside includes winding roads, active farms, miles of woodlands, antique buildings, and quintessential New England villages. There is a good collection of high quality antique dealers in the area specializing in everything from jewelry to furniture. Naturalists and outdoor enthusiasts can choose from a wide range of seasonal activities.

Innkeepers Birdie and Ken Olson retired to Thompson and built Hickory Ridge as their home and a bed and breakfast in 1990. Situated on three gently sloping acres bordering on Quaddick Lake, the inn provides serene views, comfortable accommodations, and warm, helpful hosts. The inn offers three rooms. We stayed in two of the rooms which shared a bath. We also had a private entrance with patio and our own sitting room with a hide-a-bed couch and a television with VCR. The Olsons maintain a video library with children's and adult titles. A family of up to six could be comfortable in this suite arrangement. A third room is available from May through October which has a double bed, private bath, fireplace, and private deck overlooking the lake. All the guest rooms are furnished with antiques and have clean, simple decors.

The upper level common rooms are comprised of a dining room with a large table flanked by a wall of windows facing toward the lake and park-like lawns and an adjoining living room with a beautiful granite block fireplace and comfortable furnishings. The building's post and beam construction makes both of these rooms feel open and inviting. Birdie provides breakfast at your convenience and generally serves a collection of homemade baked goods, including her wonderful scones, fresh fruits, and an entree of your choice.

While you are at the inn, you may spend time playing in the water's sandy beach area or go for a spin in the canoe available for guest use. Ken is often available for anyone interested in a little fishing expedition out on the lake. Guests may also enjoy bicycling, hiking, cross-country skiing, antiquing, tennis, and golf in the surrounding area. The Olson's have two bicycles for their guests to use and also offer discounts on green fees at a new course within three miles of the inn. Hikers will enjoy access to over seventeen private acres and miles of bordering state lands. Quaddick State Park is also very close by. Plan to spend a day or two at Hickory Ridge and you will come to know and like these wonderful innkeepers and the inviting hostel they've created.

Accommodations: 3 guest rooms sharing two baths. Roll-aways, booster seat, high chair, and crib available.

Rates: $50-$85, double occupancy, B&B. Additional persons, $20-$30. Discounts available for stays of longer than two days.

Methods of Payment: Cash, traveler's check, personal check.

Dates of Operation: Open all year.

Children: Appropriate for all ages.

Activities/Facilities: Swimming, boating, hiking, barbecue and picnic tables available on premises. Antique and craft shops, tennis, golf, and cross-country skiing available nearby. Historic Sturbridge Village is within 25 minutes drive and Mystic Seaport, Foxwoods, and Newport, Rhode Island are less than an hour away.

Maine

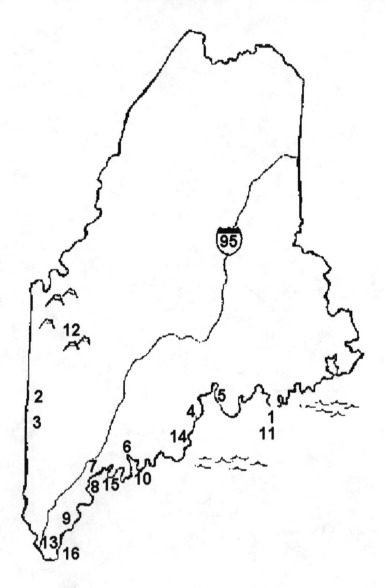

Contents

Pachelbel Inn

Innkeepers:Helene and Russell Fye
Telephone: (207) 288-9655
Address: 20 Roberts Avenue
*   Bar Harbor, ME 04609*

Bar Harbor is a quaint yet bustling town located scenically on Mt. Desert Island at the edge of Frenchman Bay. It is the primary access point to the splendors of Acadia National Park and a wealth of wonderful family activities. The Pachelbel Inn, located on a quiet residential street near both the waterfront and the downtown shopping and dining district, is a perfect base from which to launch your vacation adventures. Helene and Russell Fye, and their children Samantha and Russ, offer warm, family-style accommodations in their beautifully maintained and comfortable home.

Six well-appointed rooms are available, four of which offer private baths. We were impressed by the simplicity, cleanliness, and brightness of all the rooms. One large room on the second floor has a queen bed and can also accommodate up to three children. It has a large private bath with a tub and a shower. There is also a large room that the Fyes have recently added in what was formerly attic space on the third floor. Skylights and windows give the room an airy feel. One room also offers a private outside entrance for those who covet a higher degree of privacy.

Public rooms are on the main floor and include a good-sized living room with lots of reading material, games, and a television. Young Russ was more than happy to help our children play video games. By the way, there's a nice new basketball hoop at the end of the driveway if your youngsters need to burn off some energy. The livingroom has plenty of comfortable furniture and feels a lot like home. The dining room adjoins the living room and is flooded by light from several south-facing windows. Helene prepares a sumptuous breakfast for all her guests. The Fyes feel that a proper bed and breakfast experience should include a bountiful morning meal. Daily features include Eggs Victorian, quiche, Blushing Bunnies, or raisin French toast. Coffee, tea, assorted breads and muffins, sausages, and fresh fruit complement the daily feature.

A hearty breakfast will serve you well as you set out on your choice of a multitude of varied activities available in the Bar Harbor/Acadia area. There are whale watching tours and numerous sailing excursions to the outer islands, horseback riding, biking, museums, hiking, historic sites, beach combing, and shopping to choose from. Acadia National Park offers a plethora of sites and activities to indulge in. We drove to the summit of Cadillac Mountain (1530 feet above sea level) and took in the spectacular panorama of ocean, mountains, and fjords. It would be easy to design an itinerary lasting an entire week without even leaving the island!

We enjoyed the friendly and comfortable accommodations at Pachelbel Inn. It is sometimes difficult to find the type of charming homeport in an attractive tourist destination that the Fyes offer. We recommend it heartily.

Accommodations: 6 guest rooms, 4 with private baths. Cribs, cots, and booster seats available.

Rates: $85-$105, double occupancy, B&B. Lower rates during off-season.

Methods of Payment: Cash, traveler's check, personal check, major credit cards.

Dates of Operation: Open all year.

Children: Appropriate for all ages.

Activities/Facilities: Full range of outdoor activities available in the area year-round. Acadia National Park is minutes away. Plenty of in-town dining, shopping, and sightseeing opportunities.

The Chapman Inn

Innkeepers: George and Sandra Wight
Telephone: (207) 824-2657
Address: *P.O. Box 206*
           Bethel, ME 04217

Bethel, Maine is a pleasant and attractive community located in the Oxford Hills along the banks of the Androscoggin River in west central Maine. Its streets are lined with fine old homes including the Chapman Inn which is located at the center of town facing the village green. Innkeepers George and Sandra Wight offer a wide range of accommodations ranging from traditional bed and breakfast to efficiency apartments and dormitory style lodging for larger groups.

The Bethel area has a lot to offer visitors during all four seasons. Summer activities include golf at an 18-hole championship course within a short walk of the inn, hiking and swimming in Grafton Notch State Park and White Mountain National Forest, and a full range of boating, fishing, and bicycling opportunities.

The inn offers guests access to its private beach located on Songo Pond, five miles away. Wintertime attractions include downhill skiing at two nearby resorts. Sunday River ski resort is six miles from Bethel and is one of Maine's major alpine and cross-country ski destinations. Mount Abram ski area is located in nearby Locke Mills and is known for well-groomed trails and a family atmosphere. Numerous cross-country and snowmobile trails are also available in the area. Bethel's historic district can be toured right from the inn by foot, bicycle, or car.

When you return to the inn, you can relax with a book or converse with the other guests in the fireplaced living room or take in the fun of the gameroom which features pool table, darts, cable television, and two private saunas. Sandra keeps a ready supply of snacks, cookies, and cheese and crackers available almost all the time. Coffee service and spiced apple cider are always available as well. A hearty breakfast is served each morning in the spacious dining room. A buffet of fruits, cereals, muffins, juices, and coffee complement a daily egg or pancake entree. The bed and breakfast guest rooms are tidy and clean. Each bed features a comfortable quilt and numerous pillows. The rooms are large and many of them have multiple beds. If you are interested in eating in, you might inquire about the efficiency apartment as well.

Accommodations: 6 B&B rooms, 4 with private baths. Numerous efficiency, apartment, and dormitory rooms also available.

Rates: $55-$95, double occupancy, B&B. Additional persons $5-$15. Efficiency apartment is $75, double occupancy, EP. Additional persons, $20. Inquire about dormitory accommodations and off-season rates. Weekly rates available.

Methods of Payment: Cash, traveler's check, personal check, major credit cards.

Dates of Operation: Open all year.

Children: Appropriate for all ages.

Activities/Facilities: Gameroom and sauna rooms available on the premises. Skiing, hiking, canoeing, golf, fishing, and swimming at private beach in summer. Skiing, snowmobiling, and winter sports available nearby. Ice skating right out the inn's front door.

The Noble House
Bed and Breakfast

Innkeepers: Jane and Dick Starets
Telephone: 207) 647-3733
Address: P.O. Box 180
*   Bridgton, ME 04009*

The Noble House Bed and Breakfast is located in Maine's Western Lakes and Mountains Region, offering its visitors diverse recreational opportunities and spectacular beauty year round. The B&B's private lake frontage on scenic Highland Lake, with canoe, foot pedal boat, hammock, picnic table, and grill for summer fun coupled with their close proximity to Shawnee Peak ski area (five miles), are testimony to the region's wealth of family activities.

Innkeepers Jane and Dick Starets welcome families of all ages to their B&B with its turn-of-the-century charm and accommodations for families of all sizes. The Senator Staples Suite is spacious with its own sitting area decked out with white wicker furniture. It has a double bed, two twin beds, and its own private bath with a double sink. Another room well suited for families is room number 8. It has a queen bed in the main room with an arch opening to a smaller room with twin beds and a private bath. For parents looking for a bit more privacy, rooms 4 and 5 are perfect. Room number 4 is beautiful with its queen brass bed, whirlpool bath, and access to a screened porch. Adjoining room number 5 has twin beds and also opens to the screened porch.

The Noble House is graced with a wide wrap-around porch and broad lawns. There's lots of room to run around or play croquet when you're not swimming or fishing at the lake. The Staret's daughter Heather, is largely responsible for the B&B's interior design. The stained glass windows are also to her credit. The formal rooms consist of the parlor and dining room. However, as is true in most homes, the lounge or familyroom gets the most traffic. The lounge is furnished with comfortable pieces, a piano, television, and VCR. The mantel on the fireplace displays photos of the Starets and their four children who are all sports enthusiasts.

The Starets provide a hearty breakfast each morning usually served buffet-style in the lounge which typically features an egg dish, pancakes, waffles, and homemade bread, muffins, and granola. Young children often choose the stairs for their eating spot. Jane usually sets up some toys so parents can linger over coffee.

Families visiting Noble House will not be at a loss for things to do. The area is rich in historic museums with few crowds as well as Saco River canoe trips, miniature golf, horseback riding, and Sebago Lake cruises. North Conway, NH is within thirty-five minutes of Noble House for the outlet shopping enthusiast.

The Starets hope that families leave their B&B a memory or two richer. We think you will.

Accommodations: 9 guest rooms, 6 with private baths. Cots and cribs available.

Rates: $70-$115, double occupancy, B&B. $15 for children in room with parents.

Methods of Payment: Cash, personal check, traveler's check, American Express, MasterCard, and Visa.

Dates of Operation: Mid-June through Mid-October. Mid-October to Mid-June by advance reservation.

Children: Appropriate for all ages. (No infants on weekends in July and August.)

Activities/Facilities: Swimming, fishing, skiing, boating, shopping, historic tours, and country fairs. Large lawn for croquet, private lake frontage with canoe and foot pedal boat, bicycles with attachable child's cart, games, books, and videos.

Whitehall Inn

Innkeepers:The Dewing Family
Telephone: (207) 236-3391
Address: P.O. Box 558
*   Camden, ME 04843*

Camden, Maine is a picturesque coastal town with lots to see and do for its many visitors. Whitehall Inn is perched on a hillside overlooking the town and Camden Harbor. Guests have been welcomed here since 1901. The inn's main building was built in 1834 as a local sea captain's home and maintains much of its nineteenth century charm and elegance today. The Dewing family has operated the inn for twenty-two years and their family style hospitality makes a stay at Whitehall relaxing and enjoyable. Ed Dewing and "Uncle" Don Chambers have been involved with the inn since the family first purchased it, but much of the innkeeping duties are now handled by Ed's sons, Chip and JC, and JC's wife Wendy. The family brings a nice variety of interests and experiences to the inn and our conversations with them were comfortable and interesting.

Whitehall Inn is representative of the charm, history, and grace that Camden is known for. All three of its buildings are listed on the National Register of Historic Places. The views from the inn and surrounding area include mountains, lakes, rivers, and Penobscot Bay; a variety of landscapes that is rare and beautiful. Guests can indulge in a seemingly endless variety of local sites and activities. Windjammer cruises are available from Camden. A weekend at Whitehall before or after a six day sail would make for a memorable vacation.

Schooners, sloops, and lobster boats are available for daily tours and motor boats and sailboats can be rented for personal explorations. Fishing enthusiasts can take their pick of salt water or fresh water angling. Camden Hills State Park, just north of town, has some good hiking trails and one can hike or drive to the summit of Mount Battie for an awesome view of the islands and waters of Penobscot Bay. Picnic grounds and a public beach are also available. Lake Megunticook is within a few miles of the inn and offers swimming, boating, and fishing. Bicycle rentals are available locally, and there are several golf courses in the area. The town of Camden is plenty worthy of exploration as well. Beautiful parks and historic buildings along the oceanside streets are mixed with a variety of antique and craft shops, museums, and quality restaurants. Cultural events ranging from outdoor concerts to art shows, and harborside festivals to local theatre productions, are constantly available from spring to fall.

After a fun-filled day of exploration, Whitehall Inn will welcome you and your family for a restful and rejuvenating night's sleep. The front desk is staffed twenty-four hours a day for your convenience. The main building's lobby areas are bright and open with beautiful Oriental rugs and casual, comfortable furnishings. Several of this building's forty guest rooms can be combined into a variety of family suite arrangements which can sleep up to five and most rooms have a private bath. Across the street are two Victorian houses, The Wicker House and The

Maine House, which each have a comfortable living room and screened porch. They offer a little more privacy and may be preferred by families with small children. Of historical interest are the old-fashioned telephones in each room. They connect to the inn's own switchboard where an outside line can be obtained. An outdoor tennis court and a shuffleboard are available for guest use, and lots of beautiful gardens and wide lawns surround the inn. Merry, the resident dog, will enjoy a game of fetch with your children on the back lawn.

Wonderful breakfasts and dinners are served in the dining room in the main building. Uncle Don has served as the inn's chef for twenty-two years and his culinary skills are well developed. Breakfast includes muffins and pastries fresh from the oven and a variety of entrees that changes every other day. Native blueberries are generously utilized in a number of dishes. Dinners include homemade soups and chowders and feature a bountiful array of extremely fresh seafood entrees as well as a chicken and beef selection.

Book a stay at Whitehall Inn and you will be tempted to make reservations for your next visit before you depart.

Accommodations: 50 rooms, 44 with private baths. Roll-aways, cribs, high chairs available.

Rates: $75-$135, double occupancy, B&B. $105-$165, double occupancy, MAP. Various EP and AP rates available.

Methods of Payment: Cash, traveler's check, personal check preferred. MasterCard and Visa accepted.

Dates of Operation: Late May to late October.

Children: Appropriate for all ages.

Activities/Facilities: Tennis, shuffleboard, lawn games, puzzles, board games, television available at the inn. Beaches, lakes, boating, fishing, hiking, bicycling, historic sites, shopping, cultural events, and golf available nearby.

The Holiday House and The Manor

Innkeepers: Paul and Sara Brouillard
Telephone: Holiday House (207) 326-4335
            Manor (207) 326-4861
Address: P.O. Box 215
            Castine, ME 04421

Paul and Sara Brouillard can offer you a choice of two beautiful family getaways in the lovely bayside village of Castine. Both The Holiday House and The Manor provide a friendly, relaxed environment for guests. The Holiday House is a cheery three story frame building with a brick red roof and pale yellow siding which sits right on the shores of picturesque Penobscot Bay at Castine Harbor. The large open yard has plenty of room for badminton, horseshoes, croquet, and even a swingset and teeter totter. There's also a small gazebo at the edge of the yard next to the rocky beach. Another attraction the kids will enjoy is the resident seagull who loves to be petted. The main floor is dominated by a large sitting room which opens to a wraparound porch and deck. There's a TV and a big fireplace in the sitting room and lots of oriental rugs throughout the inn. Children are more than welcome here as evidenced by tot-size chairs scattered about and a small rocking horse next to the couch. There is a total of ten guest rooms including a cozy cottage out back with a kitchen and a porch that extends over the water's edge. Most rooms have private baths and adjoining rooms can be combined to create family suites. The rooms are all large, airy, and comfortable. A relaxed atmosphere permeates The Holiday House and we felt sincerely welcome. Breakfast is served in another large room adjoining the sitting room downstairs with a panoramic view of the bay. The buffet style continental fare typically includes a variety of quiches, muffins, fruits, cereals, and homemade preserves. And, of course, high chairs and booster seats are available.

The Manor offers a more refined atmosphere, but maintains the same relaxed, friendly air. It is located about a mile inland of Holiday House and sits on a hill with a huge sweeping front lawn. From the front door, guests can look across the lawn to the trees and town below and to the bay in the distance. As we pulled in the driveway, we knew we had found a winner. A small sign beside the drive cautions guests to "Drive Slowly, Children at Play." The inn looks somewhat like a European chalet with large gables and dormers, stone chimneys and porch pillars, and shingled siding. The main entry hall and large front room are bright and airy. A huge fireplace graces one wall and offers guests a warm welcome when the weather is cold.

Fine dining is a hallmark at The Manor. Paul Brouillard is an accomplished and attentive chef. His dinner menu changes daily and features game, fish, and foul indigenous to the area. There is also an impressive green marble and mahogany oyster bar on the front porch. A multitude of refreshments and luscious hors d'oeuvres is available daily.

The guest rooms are very generous in proportion with lots of closet space, and most have large private baths.

The Castine area offers lots of great family activities. Whether you stay at The Holiday House or The Manor, your choices include harbor tours and seal watching cruises, maps for hiking along the shores of the Castine Peninsula, cross-country ski touring during the winter, day trips to Acadia National Park, privileges at the Castine Country Club, tours of the Maine Maritime Academy, museums, shops, and much more. The Brouillards are warm and gracious and their establishments reflect these attributes. If you visit here once, chances are you'll look forward to a return visit. We do.

Accommodations: The Holiday House: 10 rooms, 8 with private baths. Cribs and high chairs available. Babysitting services available with adequate notice. Adjoining rooms can be arranged. Cottage with kitchen.

The Manor: 12 rooms, 10 with private baths. Cribs and high chairs available.

Babysitting services available with adequate notice.

Rates: The Holiday House: $75-$115, double occupancy, B&B, high season. $55-$95, double occupancy, B&B, low season. Small charge for extra persons and cribs.

The Manor: $65-$135, double occupancy, B&B, high season. $45-$115, double occupancy, B&B, low season. Small charge for extra persons and cribs.

Methods of Payment: Cash, traveler's check, personal check, MasterCard, Visa, Diners Club.

Dates of Operation: The Holiday House: April through October. The Manor: Open all year.

Children: Appropriate for all ages.

Activities/Facilities: Tours of historic sites and the Maine Maritime Academy. Beaches, golf, tennis, hiking, picnicking, harbor tours, charter sailing, seal watching cruises, museums, and waterfront shops and restaurants. Day trips to Acadia National Park. Parlor games and television.

The Brannon-Bunker Inn

Innkeepers: Jeanne and Joe Hovance
Telephone: (207) 563-5941
Address: H.C.R. 64 #045
*   Route 129*
*   Damariscotta, ME 04543*

Jeanne and Joe Hovance's warm and unassuming personalities permeate The Brannon-Bunker Inn. This quaint, clean inn is a great place for traveling families to set up a home base for their excursions to the many sites and attractions in the area. Originally built in the 1820's as a rural farmstead, the barn building was converted to a dance hall in the 1920's, and was remodeled as a roadside inn in the 1950's. Together with an adjacent carriage house, The Brannon-Bunker Inn now offers eight guest rooms and lots of down home hospitality. Jeanne and Joe have owned and operated the inn since 1984 and are raising their three children in this beautiful country setting. Jeanne is friendly and gracious and Joe is warm and laid back. Both are wonderful conversationalists and we enjoyed our talks

Maine

about topics ranging from antique collecting to politics. Joe seemed always to be involved in some topical discussion with guests. It is often the case that the personality of innkeepers is what separates a great inn from a good one. The Hovances make Brannon-Bunker a great inn.

The inn's main floor is made very cozy by a low ceiling and casual decor. The small lobby area borders a wide staircase leading to the second floor guest rooms and a small hallway leading to the public rooms at the back of the building. A breakfast area, a small `publyk' room, and an adjoining sitting area cover the length of the building and the entire space is open and convivial. A large fieldstone fireplace dominates the room. There is also a large guest kitchen just off the sitting area where visitors who want to dine in can prepare a meal. It's also a good place for baby bottles and picnic supplies. Board games and some good books are available. A color television and a box of toys are located in the sitting room for the children to enjoy. Our kids watched `Sesame Street' while we enjoyed a second cup of coffee and the ever present lively conversation. Breakfast is major continental featuring juices, coffee, tea, cold cereals, and homemade muffins. We enjoyed some of the largest, juiciest strawberries we'd ever seen. At the top of the stairs is another sitting area prominently decorated with World War I memorabilia, reflecting Joe's interest in the era. Be sure to swing by the antique shop located next door to see more of Joe's military artifacts as well as some fine Victorian furniture and lots of collectibles.

One guest room is located on the main floor and has a queen bed and a private bath. We were able to fit a roll-away bed and a crib as well. Four rooms are located upstairs, two sharing a bath and two with private bath. All the inn's rooms are deliberately old-fashioned and comfortable. Stenciled walls, handmade quilts, and country accessories create an inviting ambiance. The carriage house across the yard contains three more guest rooms including a suite with a full bath, living room, kitchen, and two bedrooms which is great for families.

54

From the screened porch on the main building, guests can enjoy a beautiful sunset over the Damariscotta River a few hundred yards west of the inn. Or you can walk down to the water's edge and catch sight of the seals playing along the shore. There is a lot to do in this coastal region including beaches, lighthouses, historic forts, quaint villages, and plenty of good restaurants. A stay at the Brannon-Bunker Inn will add to your enjoyment of this beautiful area.

Accommodations: 8 guest rooms including a family suite. 6 rooms with private bath and 2 with shared bath. Roll-aways, cribs, high chair available. Handicapped accessible.

Rates: $55-$65, double occupancy, B&B. Children in rooms with parents, $5. Extra adult, $10. Suite is $70-$115, B&B, for up to four persons.

Methods of Payment: Cash, traveler's check, personal check, MasterCard, Visa.

Dates of Operation: Carriage house is open all year. Main building guest rooms available April through November.

Children: Appropriate for all ages.

Activities/Facilities: Tennis, golf, ocean beach, lighthouse, historic fort, sightseeing, water sports, harbor and island cruises, many good restaurants, antique and craft shops available nearby. Minutes away from Wiscasset, Boothbay Harbor, and Camden activities.

The Bagley House

Innkeepers: *Susan Backhouse*
             Suzanne O'Connor
Telephone: *(800) 765-1772*
Address: *1290 Royalsborough Road*
           Durham, ME 04222

The Bagley House is situated just six miles from Freeport Maine's bustling outlet shopping. Its close proximity to Freeport and quiet country setting make it a perfect family getaway. Built in 1772, the Bagley House was originally built as an inn. The house is the oldest one in town and has a colorful and interesting history. Your kids may be interested to know that it once served as a school house. The original owner and builder, O. Isreal Bagley, opened the area's first store here and his "public house" served as the center of town in Revolutionary War days.

Innkeepers, Susan Backhouse and Suzanne O'Connor, the "two Sues," both former nurses, are always at the ready to greet their guests. With a combined count of twenty-six nieces and nephews, families will find their hosts patient and willing to accommodate their special needs. The inn has a picnic table and barbecue grill for use during warmer months and a cozy dining room for families who wish to do "take out," where you'll also find a cookie jar that's always full.

Five guest rooms, each furnished with antiques or beautifully crafted custom pieces, feature handsewn quilts, antique table covers, and private baths. The best room for families is the Cozy Nook. It has two beds, one double and one three-quarter. It can also accommodate a porta-crib. The little windows and Beatrix Potter figurines add a whimsical touch to comfort and help your kids feel at home.

Breakfast is served in the kitchen where guests gather around an eight-foot antique baker's table. The kitchen's original huge brick beehive oven is the focal point and on cool mornings is lit to take the chill off. Fresh fruit, homemade muffins, Scottish shortbread, blueberry sourdough pancakes, farm-made sausage, and maple syrup are sumptuous mainstays of the two Sues' breakfast menu.

Many guests of the Bagley House have come to the area for one reason—to shop. However, the surrounding area is chock-full of wonderful adventures. Your innkeepers are well versed on Audubon nature trails, secluded picnic spots, the best places to view Maine's famous lighthouses, sparkling clean beaches, cross-country ski trails, and berry picking in summer.

In residence is an all-American white/buff shephard/lab named Shasta Daisy. She shares the inn with the hundred-odd penguins tucked into the nooks and crannies of the house. The "two Sues" love for their home and committment to innkeeping have created an atmosphere your family will surely enjoy.

Accommodations: Five guest rooms, all with private bath. Crib, cot, and high chair available.

Rates: $85-$115, double occupancy, B&B.

Methods of Payment: Cash, personal check, traveler's check, American Express, Discover, MasterCard, and Visa.

Dates of Operation: Open all year.

Children: Appropriate for all ages.

Activities/Facilities: Shopping and beaches close by. Hiking and cross-country skiing from inn's back door. Many books, games, and puzzles. Computer and fax also available.

The Isaac Randall House

Innkeepers: Jim and Glynrose Friedlander
Telephone: (207) 865-9295, (800) 865-9295
Address: 5 Independence Drive
*   Freeport, ME 04032*

Freeport, Maine is an outlet shoppers haven of worldwide renown. But it also offers easy access to a wide variety of coastal Maine's best outdoor activities. The Isaac Randall House sits proudly on five well groomed acres within a stone's throw of the primary outlet shops. If your vacation plans include a healthy dose of outlet browsing mixed with ocean, beach, and inland excursions, you will enjoy the central location of this splendid 1823 farmhouse. The inn's grounds offer plenty of room to play or wander through the woods to the spring-fed pond.

The Friedlanders have created a warm and welcoming hostel for traveling families. Eight air-conditioned rooms offer a variety of configurations suitable to any size family. Several rooms offer multiple beds and all have private baths. Room decors vary widely and feature period furnishings, copper tubs, or varied historical artifacts. All rooms are decorated with fresh flowers and Crabtree & Evelyn toiletries. Nightly turn-down service, bedtime mints, and vintage linens add the personal touch that makes every visitor feel special.

The comforts of home and the pleasure of new found friends can be enjoyed in the sitting room. Chess and a variety of other games, cable television, and a VCR with a collection of good movies including children's titles, comingle with cozy coversation areas to give everyone a place to relax. There's also a second kitchen for guest use, a real convenience for those traveling with small children or the hopeless midnight snacker.

Breakfast is served each morning in the bustling kitchen with its nineteenth century beams, hanging copper pots and long wooden trestle table. Jim's breakfasts feature a regular rotation of entrees including orange-almond French toast, blueberry pancakes, huevos rancheros, omelets, sour cream waffles, and quiche. A variety of juices, homemade breads and granola, yogurt, cottage cheese, and seasonal fresh fruit round out the offerings. To leave the table hungry is to miss one of the primary joys of a stay at Isaac Randall House.

In addition to shopping at L.L.Bean and all the other distinctive shops, local excursions could include hiking at nearby Wolf Neck Woods State Park, a tour of the forty acre Desert of Maine, or a visit to the Mast Landing Sanctuary of the Maine Audubon Society. Bay cruises, deep sea charters, and junkets to Eagle Island would also make for fun family outings. The classic New England hospitality of the Friedlanders and the abundance of local sites and attractions will make a visit to The Isaac Randall House a pleasurable experience for your family.

Accommodations: 8 guest rooms, all with private bath and air conditioning. Crib and high chair available. Several rooms can be combined to form family suites.

Rates: $90-$125, double occupancy, B&B. Lower rates during off-season. $15 for extra persons in room.

Methods of Payment: Cash, traveler's check, personal check, MasterCard, and Visa.

Dates of Operation: Open all year.

Children: Appropriate for all ages.

Activities/Facilities: Games, cable television, children's movies, outdoor barbecue grill, swingset and sand box, wooded trails, ice skating, cross-country skiing available on premises. Distinctive shopping, a multitude of dining options, ocean activities, beaches, cultural events, historical sites, and family entertainment available in immediate vicinity.

The Maine Stay Inn

Innkeepers: Carol and Lindsay Copeland
Telephone: (207) 967-2117, (800) 950-2117
Address: 34 Main Street
P.O. Box 500A
Kennebunkport, ME 04046

Carol and Lindsay Copeland are the latest in a long line of innkeepers at The Maine Stay Inn. Guests have been welcomed to this beautiful 1860 house since 1941. The Copelands arrived in 1989 and have created a peaceful getaway for couples, honeymooners, and families. Located in Kennebunkport's historic district, the inn reflects the seafaring genesis of the area and is listed on the National Register of Historic Places. Eleven all-season cottages, four with fireplaces, surround the main building and offer private, comfortable accommodations for families. Two suites in the main building would also work well for families. The inn's grounds are spacious and well tended. A large lawn area behind the main building features a collection of comfortable lawn furniture, a barbecue grill for guests to use, and a wooden gym and swingset nestled in a sandy area between towering pines. The side yard has beautiful gardens, an arbor, and another large lawn area where the croquet set is usually set up.

The main building has a beautiful wraparound porch with wicker furniture where guests can enjoy their breakfast or take in the Copeland's wonderful afternoon tea service in the summertime. Main floor common rooms include a dramatic living room and a beautiful dining room furnished with a large communal table and antique sideboards and accessories. The living room features a gorgeous black, peach, and green floral carpet with overstuffed, chintz covered chairs and couches. Chandeliers, formal window coverings, and lots of impressive, heavy woodwork give the entire inn a warm, Victorian feel. Don't miss the crystal sunburst windows in the living room. The suspended spiral staircase is also an impressive architectural feature.

Guest rooms in the main building have high ceilings, elegant wallpaper, and antique, wicker, and period furnishings. A first floor suite includes a queen bed, separate living room with sleeper couch, a fireplace, and a private bath. There is also a suite on the second floor with similar accommodations but no fireplace. All of the inn's rooms, including the cottages, have cable television. Most of the cottage rooms have multiple beds and full kitchens. Number Six has a double bed, two twin beds in a second bedroom, plus a twin sleeper in the living room couch. The decor in the cottage rooms is decidedly more casual than the main building rooms, but the Copeland's have done a nice job of updating them with modern carpeting, fresh paint, and wicker and antique metal beds.

A full breakfast is served every morning and cottage guests can make arrangements to have their breakfast delivered to their room in a basket. This was a great option for us, as we leisurely enjoyed our breakfast while baths and dressing rituals were in progress. If you choose to eat in the dining room, you will enjoy a beautifully set table and well-presented dishes. Fresh fruits, homemade sweet breads, English muffins, juices, and coffee complement a daily entree such as baked French toast, blintz souffle, or Serbian eggs which is a tasty ham, cheese, and egg dish.

Plenty of interesting activities are available in Kennebunkport and the surrounding area. Beaches, bicycle rentals, and golf at several area courses are popular warm weather attractions. Hot air balloon rides and several amusement centers are available all year. We recommend blueberry picking in August and there are several orchards where autumn apple picking is fun for the whole family. Shopping and sightseeing are plentiful around town and up and down the coast. A Christmas Prelude festival and several other local seasonal events are worth inquiring about.

The Copelands' gracious hospitality and beautiful accommodations, and the scenic surroundings of Kennebunkport and the Maine coast, will make your stay a pleasurable one.

Accommodations: 17 guest rooms including 6 rooms in the main building and 11 cottage rooms, all with private baths. Suite accommodations available in main building and cottages. Roll-aways, cribs, high chair available.

Rates: $85-$195, double occupancy, B&B. Children under 3 years are free; ages 4 to 11 years, $8; 12 years and over, $20. Small fees for roll-aways and cribs.

Methods of Payment: Cash, traveler's check, personal check preferred. MasterCard, Visa, American Express accepted.

Dates of Operation: Open all year.

Children: Appropriate for all ages.

Activities/Facilities: Lawn games, swingset, barbecue grill, afternoon teas at the inn. Golf, fishing, bicycling, ocean and whale watching tours, hot air balloon rides, family attractions, shopping, sightseeing, access to private beach with beach parking permits, towels, and umbrella. Cultural activities available nearby.

The Bradley Inn

Innkeepers:Chuck and Merry Robinson
Telephone: (207) 677-2105
Address: Route 130
*   H.C. 61*
*   361 Pemaquid Point*
*   New Harbor, ME 04554*

Majestically set on three acres a short walk from Pemaquid Point, the inn seems to beckon weary travelers. The majority of the property lies in front of the main building and is landscaped with beautiful flower gardens, isolated groves of trees, and large, manicured lawns. Nestled amongst the trees, bushes, and flowers are several settings of lawn furniture and a beautiful covered gazebo. Croquet is popular with guests and we can't imagine a more appropriate venue.

The inn's main building is a large, three story turn-of-the-century structure. Several outdoor patios and canopies grace the entrances and add to the appeal of the surrounding grounds.

Indoors, the main lobby area and adjoining hallways are bright, open and cleanly decorated. Floral print chairs and couches combine with lots of beautiful light wooden trim and accents to create a friendly and pleasant gathering place. Innkeepers, Merry and Chuck's maritime collection of books and art are quite impressive and are placed throughout the common rooms of the inn. The Pub with its oversized bar adjoins the Chart Room where the atmosphere is rather cozy with its wood burning stove. The Living Room is more formal and houses a baby grand piano.

There are twelve guest rooms located in the main building and a cottage tucked away in a private corner of the property as well as a carriage house that overlooks the gardens. In the main building, nine rooms have queen beds and three have twins. All rooms have private baths. Two rooms are located at the end of a downstairs hallway and can be combined to create a family suite with two baths. The cottage has a bedroom with queen-size bed, living room with fireplace, television, and two daybeds, bathroom with shower and fully equipped kitchen. The carriage house consits of two floors. The top floor suite has a bedroom with a queen-size bed and a sleeping loft with two twin beds, a full bath, kitchen and dining area. The living room has cable television and a private phone. Downstairs are two additional bedrooms and two more bathrooms. It's perfect for a large family. Each guest room is furnished comfortably and attractively. Many command views of John's Bay.

The Pemaquid area offers lots of summer activities well suited to families. Bike riding, canoeing, fishing, and hiking are popular. Pemaquid Beach is three miles from the inn and Pemaquid Point, lighthouse and all, is less than a five minute walk. Other nearby attractions include boat trips to Monhegan Island and the fascinating tidal pools of the Rachel Carson Salt Pond.

Inn guests can enjoy a hearty continental breakfast. (Cottage and carriage house guests need to add an additional $5.00 per person per day.) But the Robinsons focus their culinary efforts in the restaurant called "Ships." Dinner offerings include seasonal native seafood dishes, and select beef, chicken, and pasta dishes. A variety of wines from California and France are available to complement your meal. Chef Jeffrey Parker, graduate of the Culinary Institute of America, prepares your evening fare.

Chuck and Merry, along with their dog Barney, a loveable and well-behaved golden retriever welcome your family to experience the beauty of Pemaquid Point at the Bradley Inn.

Accommodations: 12 rooms in main building, all with private bath. Roll-aways and crib available. Cottage sleeps four and is rented by the week. Carriage house sleeps eight and is also rented by the week.

Rates: $90-$155, double occupancy, B&B. Additional person, $20. Cottage $650, Carriage house $975 per week during peak season.

Methods of Payment: Cash, traveler's check, personal check, major credit cards.

Dates of Operation: Approximately Memorial Day to Thanksgiving.

Children: Appropriate for all ages.

Activities/Facilities: Large, completely renovated building in private location. Lawn games, biking, walking, fishing, boating. Beach and light house within short distances. Many local attractions including the Rachel Carson Salt Ponds.

The Maison Suisse Inn

Innkeepers: Beth and Dave White
Telephone: (207) 276-5223, Reservations (800) 624-7668
Address: Main Street, P.O. Box 1090
*   Northeast Harbor, ME 04662*

Acadia National Park is a combination of breathtaking ocean, lake, and mountain scenery. The twenty-two square miles of Mount Desert Island that form part of Acadia is a geologic wonder. Ice-age glaciers and the relentless pounding of the ocean surf have created this landscape of valleys and islands. Northeast Harbor, on beautiful Mount Desert Island, offers visitors an unhurried atmosphere. It is considered to be the most enchanting of Acadia's villages.

The Maison Suisse Inn was originally built as a summer cottage in the late nineteenth century. The inn commands a handsome presence along Northeast Harbor's main street of shops and restaurants. Its name was given by a former owner from Switzerland who cultivated the gardens still enjoyed today.

Many of the village's attractions are within walking distance from the inn. Golf, tennis, swimming, a botanical library, three public gardens, a small museum of local history, and the public library are all nearby.

The inn's fireplaced common rooms and ten guest rooms and suites capture the essence of a grand turn-of-the-century manor. The guest rooms are furnished with beautiful antiques and other fine pieces. The decor is graceful and uncluttered. The inn offers a variety of accommodations. The two room suites are ideal for families. In one of the suites there's a queen canopy, a double, and a twin bed. In the octagonal suite with fireplace, there's a queen bed, an extra long twin, and a double day bed. One of the smaller rooms has a queen bed with a bay window, in which a twin fouton can be placed. A king bedded room with its own porch has a twin day bed. Cots and cribs are also available.

Breakfast is provided at a restaurant (with on-site bakery) right across the street from the inn. This gives families the ultimate in flexibility with service from seven to eleven each morning. You can choose a full breakfast of eggs, bacon, and homefries or continental fare of cold cereal and breakfast pastries. There is truly something for everyone.

After a good night's rest and a hearty breakfast your family should be recharged and ready to take in the sights of Acadia. The park's fifty-seven miles of carriage trails can be explored on foot, horseback, or bicycle. Sailing, whale watching excursions, and ferry boats can be launched from many of the island's harbors. Nearby Bar Harbor provides abundant opportunities for shopping, dining, and entertainment.

The Maison Suisse Inn's gracious hospitality combined with Acadia's unspoiled beauty will no doubt make for lasting family memories.

Accommodations: 10 guest rooms and suites, all with private baths.

Rates: $105-$165, double occupancy, B&B. Two room suites, $175-$205, double occupancy, B&B. Additional guests in same room (over 18 years old) are $15 per night. Children are $10 per night in same room as parents. Please call for off-season rates.

Methods of Payment: Cash, personal check, traveler's check, MasterCard, and Visa.

Dates of Operation: Mid-May through October.

Children: Appropriate for all ages under caring adult supervision.

Activities/Facilities: Boating, fishing, whale watching, golf, tennis, swimming, shopping, hiking, bicycling, and horseback riding.

The Rangeley Inn

Innkeepers: Ed and Fay Carpenter
Telephone: (207) 864-3341, (800) MOMENTS
Address: P.O. Box 160
           Rangeley, ME 04970

If your family enjoys active outdoors oriented vacations and you're tired of crowds and cutesy resorts, Rangeley, Maine might be just what the doctor ordered. Tucked away in the Western Mountains and Lakes Region, the area offers a wide range of outdoor activities all year long. The Rangeley Inn serves as a center of activities and offers wonderful accommodations for families.

Ed and Fay Carpenter have owned the inn for twenty-two years and provide guests with comfortable, friendly service aided by daughter Janet, and an attentive outgoing staff. The inn's main building is an imposing three story structure with a wide front porch overlooking Rangeley's quiet main street. One section of the building dates to 1877, but most of the current inn was built in 1907. Rangeley was a popular summer destination for people from large cities all over the northeast in the early twentieth century. In those days, The Rangeley Inn served as a summer residence for city dwellers drawn to the cool fresh air and clean water that dominates the area. Today it offers guests a warm and homey getaway for a day or a week throughout the year. Located on seven acres bordering Haley Pond, a bird sanctuary, the inn has lots of room to roam. A large lawn out back is replete with lawn furniture, trees, and a great view of the pond and surrounding hills.

Fifty-one guest rooms are divided between the main building and a more modern motel unit with pond frontage. All rooms are large and roomy. Each room is furnished with antique furniture and provides a full, private bath. In the main building, many rooms have multiple beds and the bathrooms are restored to their turn-of-the-century decor. And the closets are huge. Ed informed us that they were built to accommodate the large steamer trunks brought by summer-long visitors in the early years of the inn. The motel rooms are more modern, but are very roomy and are also furnished with antiques. Some also include jacuzzis, or wood stoves popular with the winter crowd. Each motel room has a private entrance which some families prefer. The common areas are large, open, and comfortable. The main sitting room has lots of couches, chairs, and tables and focuses on a beautiful fireplace and an old horse-drawn sleigh tucked in the corner. There's also a separate entertainment room next to the lobby with a TV, VCR, games, and books. It's not unusual for these rooms to be filled with children making new friends and playing together.

The newest addition to the Carpenters' repetoire of accommodations is the house adjacent to the main inn. Formerly a single-family residence, the house has been thoroughly renovated and is available for daily or weekly rental. It includes two baths, living area, kitchen, and can sleep up to ten people.

Ed and Fay are very friendly and talkative and the warmth of their hospitality permeated our stay. Innkeepers create an atmosphere that reflects their personalities and the Carpenters have created a getaway that embodies their own unpretentious friendliness. Ed toured the property with us and had countless stories to tell of the history of the inn and the various intricacies of the building. Ask him about the pressed tin ceiling in the dining room. He even gave us an interesting tour of the furnace room. With his training as an engineer, he has incorporated several unique, energy saving features of which he is justifiably proud.

There is more than enough to do in the area for any active family. Boating, fishing, hiking, swimming, biking, and golf are readily available in summer. And wintertime activities include downhill skiing at nearby Saddleback Mountain, cross-country skiing, ice skating, snowmobiling on a network of trails accessible directly from the inn, and even dog sled racing. The inn is one block from a town park with a boat dock on Rangeley Lake and innumerable activities are available on the lakes and ponds and in the mountains nearby. Of particular interest are the early morning canoe trips offered at the inn. They are very popular with guests who almost always get to view wild moose along with countless other wildlife in a pristine and beautiful setting.

Guests are welcome to take their meals in the restaurant located in the inn. The breakfast menu offers a variety of entrees ranging from porridges to eggs and several waffle and pancake selections. We especially enjoyed the fresh peach waffles. The dinner menu includes a varying selection of meat, fish, and pasta dishes. Baked stuffed sole, blueberry chicken, and rib eye steak are a typical sampling. Rooms at The Rangeley Inn are offered on and EP or MAP basis, so you can choose to include your meals with your room or pay only for the meals you take at the inn.

We enjoyed our stay with the Carpenters and feel confident that their warm hospitality will provide your family with an enjoyable experience as well.

Accommodations: 51 rooms in the main inn and motel unit plus the cottage building next door. Cribs, high chairs, and booster seats available.

Rates: $69-$109, double occupancy, EP. $68-$83, per person, double occupancy, MAP.

Methods of Payment: Cash, traveler's check, personal check, MasterCard, Visa, American Express.

Dates of Operation: Open all year. No meals served December 1 to Christmas and April.

Children: Appropriate for all ages.

Activities/Facilities: Game/TV room in main building, televisions in motel unit rooms, large lawn for picnics and play. Skiing, biking, hiking, swimming, boating, fishing, golf, snowmobiling available in the immediate proximity.

Academy Street Inn

Innkeepers: *Edie and Tom Boogusch*
Phone: *(207) 384-5633*
Address: *15 Academy Street*
South Berwick, ME 03908

Academy Street Inn sits as a graceful backdrop to a charming
New England town square. This grand Colonial style Victorian
is a masterpiece of fine craftsmanship from a bygone era.
Innkeepers Edie and Tom Boogusch have lovingly restored the
inn to its original grandeur of carved fireplaces, oak wainscoting, wood floors, Austrian crystal chandeliers, and leaded glass
windows.

The inn's five guest rooms are large and comfortably furnished.
All of the rooms are inviting and warm with coordinating comforters, window coverings, and wallpaper. The Navy room has a
double, and a twin bed with plenty of room for a cot. Two additional spacious rooms can open to create a family suite. All the
guest rooms have private baths.

A hearty breakfast is served in the elegant dining room, on the screened porch, or out on the deck. Native Maine blueberry pancakes, eggs, and sausage, French toast, Edie's homemade cinnamon bread and blueberry muffins are the inn's standard fare and are sure to rouse even the soundest sleeper.

On those busy mornings, Edie and Tom get help from their two youngest children, Andrew, twelve, and Kelsey, eight. During college vacations, Jeremy, 22, and Shawn, 19 return home and help out as well. The inn is also home to Honey, a very friendly golden retriever.

Academy Street Inn's location in Maine's South Coast Region lends itself to many opportunities for family fun. Berwick's gentle sloping farmland is perfect terrain for bicycling enthusiasts. York Beach, picturesque Portsmouth, New Hampshire, and abundant outlet shopping in Kittery are all within a thirty minute drive.

Berwick is also home to The Hackmatack Playhouse featuring real "olde time" summer stock theatre.

Accommodations: Five guest rooms, all with private bath. Cot and high chair available.

Rates: $45-$60, double occupancy, B&B. $10 for additional person in same room.

Methods of Payment: Cash, personal check, traveler's check.

Dates of Operation: Open all year.

Children: Appropriate for all ages.

Activities/Facilities: Bicycling, shopping, beaches, and historic tours nearby. Playground across the square from inn.

The Craignair Inn

Innkeepers: Terry and Norman Smith
Telephone: (207) 594-7644
Address: Clark Island Road
*   Spruce Head, ME 04859*

Rooted in the history of granite quarrying days of the early twentieth century, The Craignair Inn offers visitors a relaxed, unpretentious getaway. The inn was built in 1928 as a boarding house for workers in nearby quarries. Clark Island, which lies just south of the inn and is connected to the mainland by a short land bridge, was the sight of several quarries. Granite from Clark Island was used in New York City's Central Park and the Library of Congress building in Washington, D.C. The houses lining Clark Island Road are mainly former quarry workers' homes. The old general store and post office and the union hall are still standing.

The inn's main building is an imposing three story structure which commands a prominent position set on approximately four acres of rocky outcropping at the water's edge. In summertime, innkeepers Terry and Norman Smith maintain a multitude of cheery flower gardens and a deceptively large lawn area extending down to the rocky shoreline. The Smiths have been Craignair's innkeepers since 1978. In 1984, they purchased the original Clark Island Baptist Church next door and converted it into eight modern guest rooms, each with separate entrance and private bath. The main building has fourteen guest rooms all with shared baths. Wood floors covered with hooked rugs add warmth to each room. Terry has sewn quilts for each bed using handmade covers stitched by local quilters. Two rooms on the top floor can be combined to create a family suite with a double bed, two single beds, and a private bath.

A large dining room and a cozy library sitting room make up the inn's first floor. The sitting room is chocked full of an eclectic mix of Victorian overstuffed couches and chairs, oriental style room screens, china cabinets, lots of books, and a variety of art deco lamps and accessory furnishings. The dining room is large, open, and bright with a panoramic view of the waterfront and about twenty spaciously arranged tables. Terry's extensive collection of delftware china decorates the entire room. Of particular interest to families with younger children is the small sitting room on the third floor. Games, books, and other amusements are available here as well as an antique wooden refrigerator for storing picnic supplies, baby formula, and the like. We thought this room would be great for parents to relax in during naps or after the children are asleep for the night.

Full breakfasts are served restaurant style to inn guests in the dining room. Several choices ranging from cold cereal to pancakes or bacon and eggs are available each morning. In the evening, the dining room is open to the public for dinner. Entrees are moderately priced and include veal, prime beef, and several French and American seafood items. Family activities in the area include walks along coastal paths adjacent to the inn, a regular visitation of seals to watch, and various water activities. When the tide is out, a large, hard sand beach makes a perfect playground for curious youngsters. Tidal pools, clam-covered rocks, seashells, and the shallow surf can provide an afternoon filled with fun and discovery. Across the land bridge and down a dirt road on Clark Island are two salt water filled granite quarries that make wonderful summertime swimming holes for Craignair guests. In winter, cross-country skiing, snowshoeing, and ice skating are available in the immediate area.

Day trips in the surrounding area include Owl's Head Lighthouse and State Park, sailing, shops and art galleries in nearby Camden and Rockland, numerous festivals and country fairs, golf, tennis, and horseback riding.

Accommodations: 14 rooms with shared bath and 8 with private bath, in Vestry. Cots are available for $15 per night, including breakfast, and cribs are available for $5 per night.

Rates: $64-$93, double occupancy, B&B.

Methods of Payment: Cash, traveler's check, personal check, major credit cards.

Dates of Operation: May through October.

Children: Appropriate for all ages.

Activities/Facilities: Ocean-front property with sandy beach area at low tide. Swimming in old granite quarries on neighboring property. Shoreline paths for hiking. Island ferries, lighthouses, state parks, museums, shopping, and skiing available nearby.

The Lawnmeer Inn

Innkeepers: Jim and Lee Metzger
Telephone: (207) 633-2544, (800) 633-7645
Address: P.O. Box 505
West Boothbay Harbor, ME 04575

The Boothbay Harbor region is one of Maine's premier destinations. The Lawnmeer Inn is tucked away at the water's edge on the serene island of Southport just minutes away from bustling Boothbay Harbor. You can enjoy the area's festivities during the day and retreat to the peace and quiet of Lawnmeer in the evening. The Lawnmeer is the oldest operating inn in this traditional New England seaport offering old-fashioned hospitality and comfortable, clean accommodations. Boothbay Harbor evolved from a working fishing village to a summer resort in the early 1900's. Museums dedicated to preserving this region's fishing heritage can be found nearby, including one in the lighthouse at Pemaquid Point.

Maine's craggy coastline offers a multitude of excursions. More than fifty daily cruises exploring the harbor and other islands are offered during the summer. Whale and seal watching cruises are very popular. If you want to get away from the hustle and bustle of Boothbay Harbor, we recommend a day trip to Monhegan Island. The Maine State Aquarium has "touch" tanks and other exhibits of marine life indigenous to the Maine coast. For a day of swimming and picnicking, innkeepers Jim and Lee Metzger will direct you to the Southport town beach on the island's west shore. They'll even pack a basket lunch for you.

The main inn, two guest wings, and a couple of cottages are conveniently arranged over five acres of lawns, gardens, waterfront, and rock outcroppings. Adirondack chairs are scattered around the lawns for guests to take in the views. While playing in the yard, our kids found a small patch of wild strawberries that they picked clean. A number of the thirty-five guest rooms would work well for families. The Metzgers have recently added a wonderful suite called the Woods House. A kitchen, dining area, living room, two bedrooms, and a bath make this a great facility for a family planning to spend a few days or more. The guest rooms in the two wings all have televisions, balconies, and private entrances. All guest rooms have private baths.

An excellent restaurant, serving both breakfast and dinner each day, overlooks the lawn and water below. A screened porch is a great place to enjoy breakfast while watching the fog lift from the water. The Inn's herb garden adds to Chef William's savory appetizers and entrees. A menu featuring seafood specialties, beef, and chicken will surely please the most discriminating palates. A children's menu is also available.

Baskets of stuffed bears scattered around the common rooms are waiting for children to embrace them. Jim told us that the bears often accompany children at meal time and bed time. If your family loves lobster and warm, friendly hospitality, then you're going to love The Lawnmeer Inn.

Accommodations: 35 guest rooms, all with private baths. Roll-aways available.

Rates: $40-$150, double occupancy, EP. Roll-away, $20. Children under 5 years, free; over 5 years, $20.

Methods of Payment: Cash, traveler's check, personal check, MasterCard, Visa.

Dates of Operation: Mid-May through mid-October.

Children: Appropriate for all ages.

Activities/Facilities: Harbor cruises, boating, fishing, bicycling, beaches, lighthouse, and marine life museums. Freeport, home of the famous L.L. Bean store and over 100 designer outlets, within an hour's drive. Boothbay Harbor's shops and restaurants within 5 minute drive.

Dockside Guest Quarters

Innkeepers: The Lusty Family
Telephone: (207) 363-2868
Address: Harris Island Road
P.O. Box 205
York, ME 03909

Dockside Guest Quarters has been welcoming guests for over forty years. The Lusty's warm and friendly brand of Down East hospitality make this a wonderful haven for traveling families. Dockside's Harris Island location affords panoramic views of York Harbor and its environs. From the inn's rambling porches and sweeping lawns peppered with flower gardens, guests can enjoy harbor craft making their way into the Atlantic.

The Dockside Guest Quarters is a small resort composed of the original homestead of the 1880's, called the Maine House, a classic large New England summer home, four multi-unit cottages, and The Restaurant-at-Dockside Guest Quarters. The Maine House is filled with nautical paintings, ship models, and old navigation maps and books. Its guest rooms are bright and clean with ocean views and porches. The cottages also boast views of the harbor and the Atlantic. Many have sitting rooms and kitchenettes with multiple beds for larger families. We couldn't help but think what a great family reunion destination Dockside would be. In fact, we were not surprised to find out that many reunions and weddings have taken place at Dockside. A pretty gazebo at the water's edge has seen many a couple tie the knot. The Restaurant-at-Dockside Guest Quarters has floor-to-ceiling windows affording each table a view of the harbor.

Innkeeping at Dockside is a family affair. David and Harriette Lusty raised their four sons here. Sons Eric and Philip along with their wives and young children have returned to take a hand in running the inn. Eric and his wife Carol are the primary innkeepers these days. They are sensitive to the issues traveling families encounter. They, too, are raising their three sons at Dockside. Philip and Anne, meanwhile, are busy managing the restaurant with their two children in tow. The senior Lustys are ever present greeting old and new guests alike.

Each morning a "continental plus" breakfast buffet is served in the Maine House. Blueberry Buckle, a Dockside favorite, fresh-baked breads, muffins, and fresh fruit can be enjoyed for a nominal charge. The Restaurant-at-Dockside Guest Quarters serves lunch and dinner and includes a menu featuring Maine lobster, and other seafood dishes, pasta, beef, and poultry. Its scrumptious fare and harbor views have made the restaurant popular with locals as well as inn guests.

The Lustys have put together a comprehensive activities guide for their guests. A full page outlining a dozen or more childrens' activities has been included. The guide exemplifies the Lusty's dedication and commitment of service to their guests. Maine's South Coast Region boasts some of New England's best outlet shopping. Kittery is within minutes of Dockside and Freeport is less than an hour's drive. Long stretches of white sandy beaches are also nearby. Various boating and water attractions including whale watching and lobstering excursions are readily available. On the premises you can enjoy badminton, shuffleboard, lawn games, and fishing. There is also a swingset and sandbox for the younger set.

Accommodations: 21 guest rooms, 19 with private baths. Cots and cribs available. Some units with kitchenettes.

Rates: $78-$147, double occupancy, EP. Additional guests $10. Cots $10, cribs $7. No charge for children 12 and under in Studios and Apartment Suites.

Methods of Payment: Cash, personal check, traveler's check, MasterCard, and Visa.

Dates of Operation: Memorial Day thru October and weekends from November thru May.

Children: Appropriate for all ages.

Activities/Facilities: Swimming, fishing, boating, shopping, and historic tours. Walking, bicycling, golf and tennis. Fine dining, lawn games, and boating available at Dockside.

Massachusetts

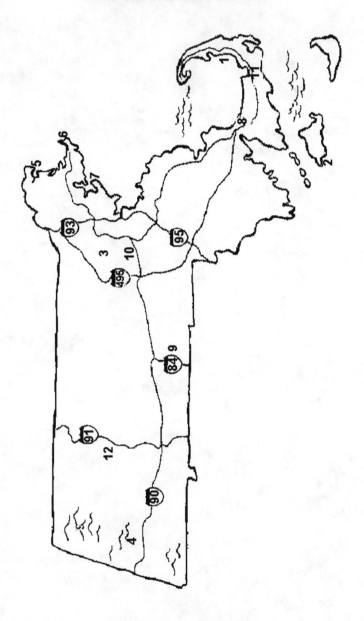

Contents

High Brewster

Innkeeper: Barbara Gullow
Telephone: (508) 896-3636
Address: 964 Satucket Road
             Brewster, MA 02631

Cape Cod is a very popular destination for summer vacations of all types. Families desiring accommodations that are quieter and slightly off the beaten path will appreciate the offerings at High Brewster. Beautifully located on over three acres of lawns and wooded areas overlooking Lower Mill Pond, the inn offers a welcome refuge from the hustle and bustle of Cape Cod in summer. Guests can enjoy the multitude of attractions and adventures in the area and return to this idyllic and tranquil setting at the end of the day.

The inn consists of four cottage buildings and the main building where the restaurant and three guest rooms are located. High Brewster is a popular dining spot for local residents and tourists. Classic American cuisine is served in three cozy dining rooms with barnboard walls, low beamed ceilings, and ladder back chairs. Inn guests enjoy continental breakfasts in the restaurant as well. Rooms in the main house reflect the country elegance of this circa 1738 structure and include private baths either in the room or down the hall.

The four cottages offer amenities that would probably be more attractive to most families with children. The Brook House has a full kitchen, two bedrooms, fireplace, and a large deck overlooking Stony Brook. The Barn Cottage is built on the site of the original barn and features one bedroom plus sleep loft with twin beds. It also has a fireplace and full kitchen. A romantic view of Lower Mill Pond is offered in the Pond Cottage, which includes one bedroom, efficiency kitchen, and screened porch. The Studio has one bedroom and a deck.

Croquet courts are usually set up on the spacious lawns in summer and a basketball hoop is available. Games, puzzles, and books are available in the main building for rainy days. Nature walks around the property are also a popular pastime. The local area offers practically unlimited opportunities for family fun. Beaches, fresh water ponds, and all sorts of boating excursions are within short distances. The town of Brewster has an interesting collection of antique shops. Nickerson State Park offers miles of trails for hiking or bicycling, and Cape Cod National Seashore is only fifteen miles away. The Cape Cod Aquarium, Museum of Natural History, and a firehouse museum are also popular local attractions.

Accommodations: 3 guest rooms with private baths. 4 private cottages. Roll-aways and high chairs available.

Rates: Guest rooms are $80-$100, double occupancy, B&B. Cottages are $100-$190 per night or $600-$1200 per week, B&B, and can accommodate up to four adults. Children under 16 are free.

Massachusetts

Methods of Payment: Cash, personal check, traveler's check, MasterCard, Visa.

Dates of Operation: Open all year. Restaurant operates daily from July 4th through Labor Day and less frequently during the rest of the year.

Children: Appropriate for all ages.

Activities/Facilities: The inn has lawn games, basketball hoop, indoor games, and puzzles. Cape Cod offers beaches, hiking, bicycling, golf, ocean cruises, museums, theatre, antiquing, tennis, and family entertainment attractions.

Breakfast at Tiasquam

Innkeeper: *Ron Crowe*
Telephone: *(508) 645-3685*
Address: *RR1, Box 296*
            Chilmark, MA 02535

Ron Crowe offers his guests an alternative to the more crowded and bustling accommodations available elsewhere on Martha's Vineyard. Breakfast at Tiasquam is quietly situated on over four acres of lightly wooded hilltop well away from the crowds and noise. This beautiful and modern bow-roofed cape features clean, open areas and twenty skylights. Eight guest rooms, two with private baths are located on both the first and second floors. A large great room is the primary common area and is also where breakfast is served. The room is awash in natural light from the plentiful skylights, windows, and atrium doors leading to a spacious patio overlooking the sloping lawns.

Guest rooms are spacious, bright, and handsomely appointed. The entire home features a high level of craftsmanship and attention to detail. Solid cherry doors, oriental rugs, custom cabinetry, and hand-thrown pottery sink basins together with beautiful hand-crafted furniture that is simple and inviting make this a wonderfully refreshing port from which to launch your island itinerary. Breakfast is a focal point for Ron and his guests. A hearty menu of seasonal offerings including fresh fish, cinnamon French toast (a house specialty), corn-blueberry pancakes, or even special requests is available each morning. Fruits, juices, coffee, and tea complement the entrees.

Inn guests can use house passes to nearby Lucy Vincent Beach or roam the property and catch a sun-dappled nap in one of the several lawn hammocks. Martha's Vineyard offers a wide variety of family activities. Bicycling is popular in the area and many island roads have designated bicycle paths. The nearby village of Menemsha is home to the island's fishing fleet and also has a public beach for swimming, shell collecting, and sun bathing. The up-island towns of Vineyard Haven and Oak Bluffs offer a wide range of dining alternatives, shops, and amusements. Ron encourages potential guests to consider a visit during the island's quiet season, November through April. The island is much less crowded during this time and favorable ocean currents keep the temperatures surprisingly moderate all year. Hiking, bicycling, and taking in the island's many natural splendors are especially enjoyable during the low season.

Accommodations: 8 guest rooms, 2 with private baths. Rollaways available.

Rates: $70-$195, double occupancy, B&B, varying by season.

Methods of Payment: Cash, personal check, traveler's check.

Dates of Operation: Open all year.

Children: Most appropriate for youngsters who no longer require cribs or high chairs.

Activities/Facilities: Beach access to Lucy Vincent Beach. Auto rental available. Dining, shopping, beaches, ocean excursions, hiking, bicycling, and numerous entertainment opportunities available in the immediate vicinity.

Hawthorne Inn

Innkeepers: Gregory Burch and Marilyn Mudry
Telephone: (508) 369-5610
Address: 462 Lexington Road
*   Concord, MA 01742*

The Hawthorne Inn is located on the famed "Battle Road" of the
Revolutionary War, where the first shots were fired in April of
1775. The inn is also situated on land once owned by Ralph
Waldo Emerson, the Alcotts, and Nathaniel Hawthorne. The
spirit of these ardent patriots and great literary minds lives on
today in the historic town of Concord.

Innkeepers Gregory Burch and Marilyn Mudry are champions
of Concord's historical significance. They produced a video
which chronicles Concord's history beginning with its Colonial
settlers in the early 1600's and ending with its present day dedication to the arts and historical preservation.

When Gregory and Marilyn started out, they were looking for a
property that they could fix up and that would be income pro-

ducing. After a long search, they found what is today the Hawthorne Inn. Their exhaustive restoration effort has produced a handsome environment. Hardwood floors, antique furnishings, and oriental rugs grace each room. Marilyn's quilts and Gregory's paintings and carvings are blended with other ancient and modern art throughout the inn. The inn's common room is tastefully decorated and is well stocked with books and magazines. A fire is laid on chilly evenings which makes it a popular place to curl up with a book. It also serves as the reception area for guests where either Marilyn or Gregory greet you with a refreshment and acquaint you with the inn. They will also give you some good dining references. An itinerary of local events and attractions is placed in each room. This is a wonderful idea and very helpful.

The inn offers seven guest rooms. Our room was large and had a fireplace and canopy bed. Each room has a private bath. Guests are served a continental breakfast of fresh fruit, wholesome home-baked breads, juices, and coffee at a common table. We lingered over coffee and conversation.

On the west side of the inn are two pine trees which Hawthorne planted. These towering pines are now in the company of hundreds of trees, bushes, bulbs, and perennial gardens Gregory and Marilyn have cultivated. The inn's grounds are spacious with lots of room for children to run around. A tree house, swingset, and sand box in the yard is where your kids will most likely meet Gregory and Marilyn's three children. Their son Ezra gave us a tour of the grounds pointing out the raspberry bushes inviting us to take a sample.

Gregory and Marilyn graciously open their inn to families and have welcomed children since long before they had any of their own. Marilyn said, "We love the energy and the love that little ones exude,"

Concord and its neighboring communities are rich with Early American history and literature. Combining history lessons with picnics and hikes through this lovely countryside will keep your kids enthused. The discovery museums in nearby Acton provide an environment of fun and learning. There are many shops and great informal restaurants in the area, too.

The Hawthorne Inn incorporates a friendly atmosphere and comfortable accommodations in a spirited, historical area.

Accommodations: 7 rooms, all with private bath.

Rates: $110-160, double occupancy, B&B.

Methods of Payment: Cash, traveler's check, personal check, American Express, Visa, Master Card and Discover.

Dates of Operation: Open all year.

Children: Appropriate for all ages.

Activities/Facilities: Literary and Revolutionary War tours. Swimming (Walden Pond), museums, wooded trails for hiking, cross-country skiing, and canoeing on Concord River. The inn's own tree house, swingset, and sandbox. Approximately 30 minutes to the center of Boston.

Rookwood

Innkeepers: Tom and Betsy Sherman, Helen Uphoff
Telephone: (413) 637-9750, (800) 223-9750
Address: P.O. Box 1717, 11 Stockbridge Road
*   Lenox, MA 01240*

Rookwood is located in the heart of the beautiful Berkshire Hills in western Massachusetts. This area is an attractive getaway for many vacationers at all times of the year. The performing arts are particularly prominent at such well known venues as Tanglewood and the Berkshire Performing Arts Theatre. Summer months are filled with the sights and sounds of music, theatre, and dance. Numerous dance and music festivals are scheduled almost every day. A visit in the fall provides the best opportunity to enjoy the region's beauty. The rolling hills, scenic villages, and vibrant foliage bring many a "leaf peeper" this way. It's also a time when numerous potters, jewelers, weavers, painters, and crafts people showcase their wares in studios and fine galleries throughout the region. There is a thriving antique trade in the Berkshires as well. Springtime brings the horticulture crowd. Flowers, trees, and plants can be viewed in abundance at Berkshire Botanical Gardens, on wildflower walks at Mount Greylock, or on various organized tours for walkers, hikers, and bicyclists. Both alpine and nordic skiing are plentiful during winter. And there are continuing presentations of dramas, comedies, and musicals at some of the local theaters.

No matter which season you choose, Tom and Betsy Sherman and Helen Uphoff will provide you with comfortable accommodations in a grand Victorian cottage at Rookwood. The inn has twenty-one rooms which present a wide range of options to visitors. We particularly liked the Turret Room, with a queen bed and a walk up in the turret to another sleeping area with a day bed. Several other rooms offer multiple beds and many have private balconies or porches. Breakfast and afternoon tea and lemonade with cookies are included in the tariff. Breakfast is continental and is served in the beautiful dining room with fireplace and trimwork and wall coverings appropriate to a Victorian home.

The other primary common room is the living room which is also of grand scale. It features another fireplace, grand piano, and a separate alcove with books and games. Comfortable furniture makes this room a natural gathering place. Rookwood is situated on a large lot with plenty of room to romp or stroll through the gardens. Or you can watch the world go by from wicker furniture on the front porch.

Accommodations: 21 guest rooms, all with private baths. Crib available.

Rates: $85-$225, double occupancy, B&B. Extra persons, $10. Rates vary by season. Weekly discount rates available.

Methods of Payment: Cash, personal check, traveler's check, major credit cards.

Children: Most appropriate for children of school age and older.

Activities/Facilities: Cultural mecca especially in summer and fall. Performing arts, crafts, antiques, And outdoor activities plentiful in the area year round.

The Clark Currier Inn

Innkeepers: Mary and Bob Nolan
Telephone: (508) 465-8363
Address: 45 Green Street
            Newburyport, MA 01950

The quintessential bed and breakfast experience can be found at
The Clark Currier Inn. Innkeepers Mary and Bob Nolan along
with their daughter Melissa, age 9, warmly welcome families to
their circa 1803 Federal style bed and breakfast establishment.
The inn boasts many original and lovely features of early nineteenth century architecture including wide pumpkin-pine floors,
Indian shutters, window seats, and an impressive original
Samuel McIntyre fireplace with elegant mantel. Another note-
able feature of the inn is the "good-morning staircase," It is truly
beautiful! An impressive array of antiques and other fine pieces
are found throughout the inn. Tasteful wallpaper, window coverings, comforters, and carpeting blend well with the inn's furnishings. The inn's common rooms exemplify the Nolans' consideration for their guests' needs. The sun-drenched garden

room is a favorite with families as it houses the inn's television and a good selection of classic family videos. Afternoon tea is also served in this cozy room looking out on the inn's lawn, gardens, and gazebo. The library is a great spot for quiet reading or a game of cards. The parlor's formal decor showcases beautifully crafted floor and ceiling moldings, built-in bookcases, the aforementioned fireplace, and fine art.

The inn offers eight lovely guest rooms all with private baths. The Pike Room with full Victorian double bed adjoins the Merrimac Room with full bed and sea captain's twin bed. Each room has a private bath and together they are ideal for families. The yard can also be accessed via a private entrance. The Hale Room offers a classic nineteenth century full-sized sleigh bed and a twin-sized sleigh bed. The handsome decor and Franklin stove make this a very special room. The Sargent Room has a double and two twin beds. The inn provides cots when needed and porta-cribs can be accommodated in most of the guest rooms.

The Nolans serve a bountiful continental breakfast consisting of fresh fruit, juice, breads or muffins, tea and coffee, and cereal in the dining room where guests join together for lively conversation, a B&B tradition.

After breakfast, slip into a pair of comfortable walking shoes and begin your tour of Newburyport right from the inn's front door. Newburyport has a rich history of boat-building and maritime trading. The town's streets are lined with beautiful homes of the seventeenth, eighteenth, and nineteenth centuries. Nearby Market Square, an historic district, offers antique stores, art galleries, eateries, and other unique shops. A short walk from the square leads to the waterfront park. Newburyport is a charming town bustling with young families and seniors alike. We found Newburyport and The Clark Currier Inn to be especially enjoyable.

Accommodations: 8 guest rooms, all with private baths.

Rates: $65-$125, double occupancy, B&B.

Methods of Payment: Cash, personal check, traveler's check, major credit cards.

Dates of Operation: Open all year.

Children: Appropriate for all ages.

Activities/Facilities: House and garden tours, craft fairs, out door concerts, whale watching, and golfing nearby. Hay rides, sleigh rides, ice skating, and a special celebration of First Night. Plum Island, the Parker River National Wildlife refuge, Boston, Salem, Gloucester, and Sturbridge Village within short drives.

Old Farm Inn

Innkeepers: Bill and Susan Balzarini
Telephone: (508) 546-3237 800-233-6828
Address: 291 Granite Street
P.O. Box 2309
Rockport, MA 01966

The Old Farm Inn is situated on the northernmost tip of Cape Ann just minutes from Halibut Point, a fifty-four acre state park, on the northern coast of Massachusetts. The inn's five acres of lawns, meadows, flowers, and woods make this seaside haven a wonderful getaway. The Balzarini family has been offering old-fashioned hospitality to their guests for over twenty years. However, their family history dates back to the early 1900's when Bill's grandfather Antone Balzarini immigrated from northern Italy. He rented the Babson Farm, now Old Farm Inn, and raised dairy cows. In 1964, Bill and his parents purchased the farm and turned it into an inn. Today Bill, his wife Susan, and mother Mabel are the primary innkeepers at the family homestead.

Country charm graces the inn with exposed beam ceilings, antiques, wide pine floors, hook rugs, and lots of quilts. Peanuts by the hearth in the sitting room and cookies in the reception area are always on hand for guests to enjoy. A hearty continental breakfast is served each morning in the cheery dining room. Sunlight drenches the room through the floor to ceiling glass windows. An array of goodies (set out on an old black iron stove) includes juice, coffee, tea, granola, cereal, homemade breads, and muffins.

Ten guest rooms tastefully decorated provide families with a variety of sleeping arrangements. The Garden Suite, with its private deck overlooks the meadow, has a queen bed and a separate sitting room with two day beds. Two rooms in the Barn Guesthouse (one with a queen and twin and one with a king) can be connected through the kitchenette to form a family suite. The Fieldside Cottage is a new addition to the inn and houses two special units. A two story apartment has two bedrooms with a full bath upstairs, and a living room, dining alcove, fully equipped kitchen, washer/dryer, and half bath downstairs. This would be a perfect spot for an extended stay. The other cottage room is spacious with a queen bed, sitting area, and large private deck. All rooms have private baths, television, and some include a refrigerator. Our kids were delighted to find a rubber duckie in the bathtub.

Rockport is a charming seacoast town. Art galleries and gift and craft shops are plentiful. Tennis, horseback riding, golf, bicycling, deep sea fishing, scenic boat rides, bird watching, antiquing, and swimming or sunning on the beaches are some of the pastimes to fill your days. Susan has put together a complete source book of things to do in the area. Treat your family to a stay at Old Farm Inn and experience the Balzarini brand of hospitality.

Accommodations: 10 rooms, all with private baths. Cribs, roll-aways, and high chairs available.

Rates: $88-$125 double occupancy, B&B. Additional person in room $10. Roll-aways, $15. Cribs, $10. Rates given by request for 2 bedroom apartment suite in the Fieldside Cottage.

Methods of Payment: Cash, traveler's check, personal check, Visa, MasterCard.

Dates of Operation: April through October.

Children: Appropriate for all ages.

Activities/Facilities: Halibut Point State Park, outdoor concerts, summer theatre, swimming, tennis, golf, bicycling, deep sea fishing, whale watch cruises, scenic boat rides, bird watching, and antiquing. Fine restaurants and shopping nearby.

The Salem Inn

Innkeepers: Diane and Richard Pabich
Telephone: (508) 741-0680, (800) 446-2995
Address: 7 Summer Street
Salem, MA 01970

Salem, Massachusetts is a quaint but bustling seaside village
steeped in history on Massachusetts' North Shore. The Salem
Inn offers accommodations reflective of that history and would
serve as a wonderful base from which to launch a fun-filled, historical family adventure. The inn comprises what formerly was
two townhouses in a handsome brick Federalist building built in
1834 by sea captain Nathaniel West and is on the National
Register of Historic Places. It offers thirty-one guest rooms featuring period detail, antique furnishings, private baths, air conditioning, telephones, cable television, and working fireplaces in
several rooms. Many of the rooms would work well for families.
We stayed in the third floor Family Suite which consisted of two
rooms plus a kitchenette and private bath. It has a king bed, a
double bed, and a sleeper sofa and easily accommodated our

family of five. Friendly touches like the basket of shampoos and soaps in our room and the candy dishes in the lobby will make all guests feel welcome and pampered. Gorgeous mantelpieces and fine woodwork together with the antique furnishings create an air of bygone elegance.

Breakfast is served in a cozy lower level room and is light continental. The breakfast room is brick-walled with several tables arranged around a fairly massive brick fireplace and oven. In warmer weather, there's also an outdoor rose garden patio where breakfast can be enjoyed.

Unless your stay is for an extended period of time, you may have a hard time choosing from the vast array of attractions in the area. Scores of museums and historical sites are within easy walking distance of the inn. The Salem Witch Museum and Salem Wax Museum headline a long list of sites which chronical the town's infamous experiences of the late seventeenth century. Seafaring history is also prodigiously displayed in the area at such establishments as the Peabody and Essex Museum and the Salem Maritime National Historic Site. Guided tours of the area are available via the Salem Trolley & Shuttle which offers one-hour narrated rounds. Boston is only eighteen miles away if you're interested in sporting events, cultural attractions, or even more history. The inn offers special Kids' Vacation Packages especially for families. Discounted rates are offered for suite accommodations and complimentary pizza and soda and passes to the Salem Witch Museum are included. Inquire with the innkeeper about availability.

Plenty of varied dining and shopping opportunities are available in the area as well. The City of Salem in cooperation with the North of Boston Convention and Visitors Bureau publishes a handy guide to local eateries, shopping areas, and attractions. It is available right at the inn and served us well in our tour of the area. A visit to The Salem Inn will indulge your family in a fascinating historical adventure. Just remember to bring your walking shoes and prepare for a happy family experience.

Accommodations: 31 guest rooms, all with private baths. Several multiple bed rooms including a two-room suite.

Rates: $89-$159, double occupancy, B&B. Extra persons, $15.

Methods of Payment: Cash, personal check, traveler's check, major credit cards.

Dates of Operation: Open all year.

Children: Best suited to children of school age and older.

Activities/Facilities: Historic seaport. Museums, historic sites, shopping, dining, walking tours, guided tours. Eighteen miles from Boston.

The Dan'l Webster Inn

Innkeepers: The Catania Family
Telephone: (508) 888-3622, (800) 444-3566
Address: P.O. Box 1849, 149 Main Street
*   Sandwich, MA 02563*

The Dan'l Webster Inn offers a combination of refined Colonial hospitality and Cape Cod attractions. Elegant accommodations and courteous service are hallmarks at the inn. The inn is located in the quaint and historic village of Sandwich, settled in 1638. The building that became The Dan'l Webster Inn was built in 1692. During the Revolutionary War the building was headquarters to local Patriots. It was later frequented by the famed statesman Daniel Webster who kept a room reserved here until 1851. Today the inn offers modern amenities while extending traditional New England hospitality.

The Catania Family purchased the inn in 1980 and launched an extensive restoration of the property. Their efforts proved to be fruitful as evidenced by the elegant accommodations and lovely grounds. Steven Catania is Vice President and General Manager at the inn, his sister Debra is Vice President of Sales and brothers Robert and Richard are Executive Chefs. The Catania's presence and strong commitment to full service has enhanced the inn's reputation as a superb country getaway.

Forty-six beautifully appointed guest rooms are available. Antiques, wood floors, and coordinating wallpaper and window coverings add to the charm of the rooms. Many of the rooms have queen canopy beds, working fireplaces and sofa sleepers. All rooms have private baths, color televisions, and telephones.

Three dining rooms specializing in American Cuisine are open to inn guests and the public. The inn has been recognized for its culinary expertise and extensive wine collection. A children's menu and portions are also available.

The inn has a wonderful source book of things to do in the area. Many attractions are in walking distance of the inn including the Yesteryear Doll Museum. Doll houses furnished in period style and old dolls beautifully costumed will delight the hearts of little girls and not too little girls. A visit to the Heritage Plantation is a must. Be sure to allow a few hours to tour this seventy-six acre landscaped estate of Americana. Cape Cod offers a wealth of activities and amusements for all. However, you may prefer to enjoy the inn's own outdoor pool and spectacular gardens and lawns.

Cape Cod is a wonderful place for family vacations and The Dan'l Webster Inn will make your stay a memorable experience.

Accommodations: 46 guest rooms, all with private baths, color television, and telephone. Roll-aways, cribs, high chairs, and boosters available.

Rates: $79-$225, double occupancy, EP. Extra persons in same room, $10, no charge if under 12 years of age.

Methods of Payment: Cash, traveler's check, personal check, Diners Club, MasterCard, Visa, Carte Blanche, Discover and American Express.

Dates of Operation: Open all year except Christmas Day.

Children: Appropriate for all ages.

Activities/Facilities: Swimming pool, conference facilities, gift shop, and 3 dining rooms at the inn. Nearby attractions include the Doll Museum, Heritage Plantation, Sandwich Glass Museum, and Plymouth Plantation. Activities on Cape Cod include, bicycling, swimming, hiking, beaches, scenic whale watching cruises, arcades, and theme parks.

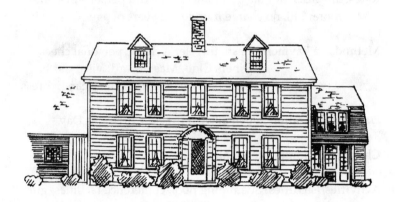

The Colonel Ebenezer Crafts Inn

Innkeeper: Shirley Washburn
Telephone: (800) 782-5425
Address: P.O. Box 187
Sturbridge, MA 01566

Old Sturbridge Village provides an authentic and friendly atmosphere in which to experience early nineteenth century life. The Colonel Ebenezer Crafts Inn, located above the village, also offers traditional Yankee hospitality combined with twentieth century amenities. Managed in association with the Publick House on the common, the Crafts Inn's accommodations are well suited for families.

This 1786 Colonial farmhouse was built by David Fiske and was more recently named in honor of Colonel Ebenezer Crafts, founder of the Publick House and an "ardent patriot" in the Revolutionary War.

Resident innkeeper Shirley Washburn welcomes guests to this gracious B&B. She has been in the hospitality industry for many years and is a native to the area. Shirley gives all her guests a tour of the inn, pointing out the lovely antique furnishings and amenities, to make your stay an enjoyable one.

Five fireplaces, located throughout the inn, enhance and warm the common areas. A large living room houses a beautiful grand piano which is complemented by the acoustics of the room. A television and VCR with a good selection of videos can be found in the library. A cheery sun porch overlooking the inn's heated pool is also a popular gathering spot for guests.

The inn offers bright, spacious, and comfortable guest rooms all with commanding views of New England countryside. Freshly baked cookies and fruit as well as plush terry robes are placed in the rooms for guests to enjoy and use. Each room is uniquely furnished with Colonial antiques and period reproductions. Two rooms in the Cottage Suite are particularly appropriate for families. These rooms provide private entrance with queen bed and queen sofa sleeper. They have been tastefully furnished by the Sturbridge Yankee Workshop. The Cottage Suite adjoins the main house via a short breezeway. A family suite in the main inn offers a queen bed and two twin beds accessible through French doors affording parents and children alike their own privacy. All rooms have private baths.

Fresh-baked muffins and sticky buns accompanied by coffee, juice, and fresh fruit along with a copy of the morning paper can be enjoyed in the dining room. Guests can also enjoy traditional Yankee cooking at the Publick House for lunch or dinner.

The main attraction in Sturbridge is Old Sturbridge Village, an authentic, rural Yankee town which has been re-created with farms, homes, a general store, and even a working gristmill. Your family will be able to experience life as it was over 200 years ago.

Admission is reasonable and will allow your family two days of enjoyment. Don't forget your walking shoes!

——————————◇◇◇——————————

Accommodations: 8 guest rooms, all with private bath. Roll-aways and cribs available.

Rates: $69-$150, double occupancy, B&B. Each additional person, $6. Roll-away or crib, $6.

Methods of Payment: Cash, traveler's check, personal check, major credit cards.

Dates of Operation: Open all year.

Children: Appropriate for all ages.

Activities/Facilities: Heated swimming pool located on the inn's grounds. Old Sturbridge Village, shops, restaurants, and attractions.

Longfellow's Wayside Inn

Innkeeper: Robert H. Purrington
Telephone: (508) 443-8846
Address: Boston Post Road
Sudbury, MA 01776

Longfellow's Wayside Inn is America's oldest operating inn. Originally built in 1702 by David Howe as a two room homestead, the inn was immortalized in 1863 by Henry Wadsworth Longfellow in his Tales of a Wayside Inn. Longfellow wrote of an "ampler hospitality" at the Wayside Inn. Today it continues to provide guests with comfortable accommodations and friendly service.

In the 1920's Henry Ford purchased the inn and generously contributed many of the inn's unique and interesting structures. The Grist Mill, an Early American reproduction, was built in 1929. The mill stone-grinds organically grown wheat and corn. Your children will be fascinated when watching the grinding process on the upper level and the mechanics in the lower level gear room. Guests can purchase the flour and meal at the inn's gift shop. The Redstone School famed by "Mary and Her Little Lamb" was built in 1798 in Sterling, Massachusetts and moved by Ford to its present location on the inn grounds in 1926. The school is now attended by the inn's "school mistress." The Martha-Mary Chapel was built in 1940 by Mr. Ford in honor of Mr. and Mrs. Ford's mothers. It is the setting for many weddings. In 1946 Henry Ford established a non-profit charitable trust. The inn presently is administered by a board of trustees dedicated to preserving the inn as a historical landmark.

Longfellow's Wayside Inn is a classic brick red clapboard building with white trim. It is surrounded by over 106 acres of New England countryside with winding roads, stone bridges and walls, cultivated fields, and a formal garden. Inside the inn you'll find priceless antiques of museum quality safely displayed in authentic viewing rooms. Guided tours of the inn can be arranged by appointment or by using a brochure for a self-guided tour.

Ten comfortable guest rooms all with private bath and air conditioning are available. Roll-aways and cribs can be added to most rooms to accommodate families. Two of the guest rooms which are reached by a steep and narrow staircase were part of the original homestead as evidenced by the gradually sloping floors and low beamed ceilings. We were told that these rooms are very popular with guests and that early reservations are a must.

The dining room which serves breakfast, lunch, and dinner can accommodate up to 130 people. Traditional Yankee fare and other specialties make this a popular spot for local residents and tour groups. Dinner reservations need to be made in advance if you choose to dine in. The atmosphere is formal yet comfortable with cloth napkins and pretty china. The wait staff dress is Colonial attire and made our special requests seem routine. Bob Purrington gave our daughter a tour of the kitchen and introduced her to the chef who made her an enormous ice cream sundae.

Our visit to Longfellow's Wayside Inn was made complete by purchasing Tales of a Wayside Inn, one of many interesting, affordable souvenirs found in the gift shop.

For a lesson in history and a brief respite, we enthusiastically recommend Longfellow's Wayside Inn.

Accommodations: 10 rooms all with private bath and air conditioning. Roll-aways and cribs available.

Rates: $65-$75, double occupancy, B&B. $10 roll-away charge.

Methods of Payment: Cash, traveler's check, personal check, Visa, MasterCard, American Express, Diners Club.

Dates of Operation: Open all year except Christmas Day.

Children: Appropriate for all ages.

Activities/Facilities: Historic sites, famous Revolutionary War landmarks, Concord and Lexington nearby. Boston 1 hour away.

Lion's Head Inn

Innkeepers: Marilyn and Tom Hull
Telephone: (508) 432-7766, (800) 321-3155
Address: 186 Belmont Road
West Harwich, MA 02671-1306

Lion's Head Inn is conveniently located near Cape Cod's south shore in a quiet residential section of West Harwich. This charming bed and breakfast establishment was originally built as a sea captain's home in the early 1800's. The inn has been beautifully restored and updated providing the modern conveniences of today while retaining the handsome features of the past.

Innkeepers Marilyn and Tom Hull are fulfilling a life-long dream as hosts of their own B&B. They have quickly become adept at their new found vocation and make all their guests feel very much at home and part of their extended family.

The inn offers six lovely guest rooms and two guest cottages. Children of all ages are welcome in the cottages. Guests eight years of age and older are also welcome in the main house. In the main inn, the Huntington Suite offers a king size bed and a day bed, providing sleeping accommodations for two additional guests. This oversized room also features a large sitting area with a couch, stuffed easy chair, and cable television, as well as a private entrance from the pool and garden areas. Each guest cottage has a living room with color television and either one or two separate bedrooms. Eat-in kitchens are fully equipped with refrigerator, electric range, microwave oven, coffee maker, toaster, and all necessary cooking utensils. All guest rooms and cottages have private baths.

The inn's spacious and well-tended grounds provide a great spot for kids to run around. Picnic tables, barbecue grills, and lawn furniture are available for cookouts and relaxation. The inn also offers a large in-ground pool and patio for guests to enjoy.

A hearty, healthy continental breakfast of fresh fruits, juices, cereals, baked goods with jams and jellies, and steaming coffee is served daily to inn guests. Breakfast can be enjoyed in the Terrace Room, at poolside, or in the quiet privacy of your own room. There is a nominal meal charge for cottage guests.

Depending on the pace your family wants to set, Cape Cod offers a wide variety of activities. Searching for seashells, digging for clams, and building sand castles on the Cape's sandy white beaches are a must. Whale watching cruises, children's theatre, miniature golf, and many, many more attractions will keep your family on the go.

Accommodations: 6 guest rooms and 2 cottages, all with private baths.

Rates: Main inn; $60-$110, double occupancy, B&B. $10 charge for each additional person in same room. Guest cottages;

The Wanderer, $575 weekly, accommodates four guests. The Morgan, $650 weekly, accommodates five guests. Discounts available during off-season. Subject to availability, cottages may be reserved for shorter stays at daily rates.

Methods of Payment: Cash, personal check, traveler's check, MasterCard, and Visa.

Dates of Operation: Main inn open all year. Cottages are closed during winter.

Children: Main inn for guests eight years and older. Cottages appropriate for all ages.

Activities/Facilities: Cape Cod offers beaches, hiking, bicycling, fishing, tennis, golf, ocean cruises, museums, theatre, antiquing. The inn has swimming pool, bicycles, lawn games, and picnic facilities.

Twin Maples

Innkeepers: Eleanor and Martin Hebert
Telephone: (413) 268-7925
Address: 106 South Street
            Williamsburg, MA 01096

Tucked away in the Hampshire Hills of western Massachusetts, you'll find Twin Maples B&B. Two towering maples, sure to be as old as the 200 year old Colonial farmhouse, serve as this charming B&B's landmark. Innkeepers Eleanor and Martin Hebert warmly welcome families to their home. They raised five of their own children here and now have four grandchildren.

Their farmhouse is very comfortable and gives one the feeling of being at home. The sitting room is cozy with antique furnishings. The wood burning stove provides guests warmth and comfort on chilly evenings. A television and VCR are inconspicuously housed behind a built-in shelving unit. We were delighted to find children's videos as part of the selection.

Twin Maples is surrounded by twenty-seven acres of unspoiled New England countryside overlooking Unquemonk Mountain. The Heberts tap their own maple trees and make their own maple syrup. You will probably want to buy a few pints to take home with you. Their flower and vegetable gardens are well tended as is the large lawn complete with picnic table. The Heberts have completely restored their farmhouse while maintaining its Colonial charm and history.

Three comfortable guest rooms, one with twin beds, two with doubles, feature restored antique beds, fresh cut flowers, and coordinating spreads and wallpaper. Our double bedded room with a fireplace comfortably fit a roll-away and a crib. When we returned for the evening we found mints on our pillows and a rag doll in our daughter's bed. All three guest rooms share a completely modern bath.

We enjoyed a full country breakfast of strawberries and cream and Eleanor's delicious walnut-cinnamon French toast. Guests can choose to eat in the beam ceilinged dining room or the screened porch.

When visiting Twin Maples you will find many things to do. Don't miss the Williamsburg General Store or Quite Plainly, one of New England's foremost country stores. In nearby Haydenville, Annie's Attic features brand name children's clothing and toys. Also nearby is Historic Deerfield home of Yankee Candle Company Many more activities can be found in the neighboring Berkshires.

Eleanor and Martin are wonderful hosts and offer their guests clean, comfortable accommodations in a beautiful setting.

Accommodations: 3 rooms, all share 1 bath.

Rates: $55-$60 double occupancy, B&B. $10 charge for roll-away or crib setup. One night surcharge, $5.

Methods of Payment: Cash, traveler's check, personal check.

Children: Appropriate for all ages.

Activities/Facilities: Nearby antique shops, general stores, and variety fairs. Skiing, bicycling, hiking, fishing, and swimming in vicinity.

New Hampshire

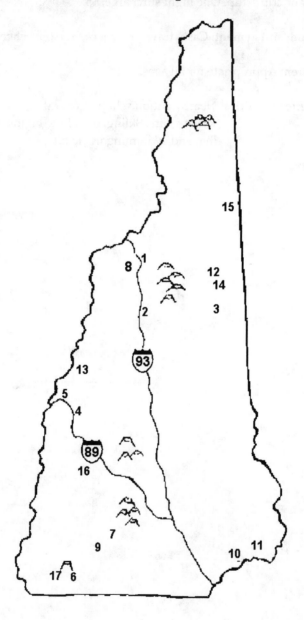

Contents

The Mulburn Inn

Innkeepers: Gary, Twila, Tim, and Lisa Skeels
Telephone: (603) 869-3389
Address: Main Street
            Bethlehem, NH 03574

You can't miss The Mulburn Inn. Its imposing presence on Main Street in Bethlehem, New Hampshire connotes an immediate feeling of welcome and warmth. The three story structure with its beautiful wraparound fieldstone porch, turreted corner rooms, and steeply pitched roof is reminiscent of the graceful grandeur of the early twentieth century. The inn's three acres are dominated by wide, manicured lawns, tidy hedges and flower gardens, and grand old hardwood trees. Built in 1913, the building was originally part of the Woolworth family estate and was the honeymoon retreat for Cary Grant and Barbara Hutton.

Gary and Twila Skeels and their son Tim and his wife Lisa operate the inn with genuine hospitality well suited to the property's history and grace. Although the Skeels are new to the inn, having purchased the property in July of 1994, they have endeavored to maintain the same friendly, family-oriented atmosphere that has always attracted us to the Mulburn Inn.

Lots of beautiful stained oak trim, high ceilings, and hardwood floors grace the inn's interior. Leaded stained glass windows, original to the building, add cheerful color to the bright and open rooms. The main floor dining room is the most impressive common room. It is a very large room with several dining tables and is lined by beautiful double-hung windows. A gorgeous fieldstone fireplace is located at one end of the room. Ornate and intricately carved woodwork covers the wall from mantel to ceiling. At the other end of the room rests a huge old white porcelain on steel stove which is also original to the building and now serves as a sideboard. The living room is comfortably furnished and features plenty of easy chairs and an entertainment center which includes a stereo, a TV with VCR, and a collection of movies for guests to enjoy. There are lots of games and puzzles, too.

A grand oak staircase leads from the living room to the seven guest rooms on the second floor. All the guest rooms are very large and comfortable with private baths. Original fixtures, period furnishings, country wall coverings, and warm wood floors add to the casual ambiance. One room features a room-sized bathroom with original ceramic tile and hot pink fixtures including a seven-foot long bath tub. There is plenty of room for cots or cribs.

Twila is the baker, while Tim is the resident chef. Twila has a collection of wonderful muffin recipes and most guests remark on her blueberry muffins. Groups of eight or more can make arrangements for a full course fireside dinner at the inn with sufficient prior notice at a very reasonable price.

A swingset and slide with jungle gym and a sandbox full of trucks, shovels, and buckets are magnetic attractions for visiting youngsters. There's plenty of room to play ball or tag. A town swimming pool just down the road is also popular with summertime visitors. Bethlehem is located at the northwestern edge of White Mountain National Forest and many family activities are easily accessible. The cog railway to Mount Washington's summit, Glen Ellis Falls, The Flume, and the Old Man in the Mountain are all just a short drive away. Hiking, biking, and fishing opportunities are also plentiful. Five golf courses are located nearby and the inn is building quite a clientele of vacationing golfers. Cross-country and downhill skiing is readily available at numerous resorts including Cannon Mountain, Bretton Woods, Loon Mountain, and Waterville Valley.

If your family vacation plans bring you to this popular north country area, a stay at The Mulburn Inn would be a fine addition to your itinerary.

Accommodations: 7 large rooms, all with private baths. Roll-aways, cribs, high chairs, and booster seats available.

Rates: $55-$80, double occupancy, B&B. $10 per extra person over four years of age. Package rates available for hikers, cyclists, golfers, and skiers.

Methods of Payment: Cash, traveler's check, personal check, Visa, MasterCard, American Express, Discover.

Dates of Operation: Open all year except Christmas Day.

Children: Appropriate for all ages.

Activities/Facilities: Outdoor games, swingset, sandbox, VCR movies, and board games available on premises. Skiing, golfing, swimming, hiking, biking, fishing, and numerous family attractions in surrounding area.

Colonel Spencer Inn

Innkeepers:Carolyn and Alan Hill
Telephone: (603) 536-3438, (603) 536-1944
Address: Campton, NH
*   RFD #1, Box 55*
*   Plymouth, NH 03264*

The Colonel Spencer Inn is an historic property, dating to the 1760's. Colonel Joseph Spencer built this house as a private residence in 1767. Innkeepers Carolyn and Alan Hill have been conducting a continuous series of renovation and restoration projects since they acquired the property and opened the inn in 1989. The result is a quaint, comfortable hostel located near many attractions and activities. Carolyn and Alan are friendly, helpful hosts who endeavored to make our stay pleasant with lots of personal attention. They had placed a collection of toys and children's books in our room before we checked in.

Six guest rooms located upstairs feature country decor, colonial color schemes, and comfortable furnishings. The Hills' eye for complementary colors and textures is evident in each room. All rooms have private baths and two rooms can be combined to create a family suite. There is also a two room efficiency suite on the main floor which sleeps up to five and is popular with families. The main floor also contains a fireplaced sitting room, a family room with television and VCR, and the large, airy dining room and kitchen. The sitting room has Indian shutters on the windows and a concealed hiding place behind the fireplace and under the stairs which were common features in pre-revolutionary structures on the frontier. Guests are served each morning in the dining room which is flooded by light from numerous windows. The kitchen area adjoins the dining room and our children enjoyed watching breakfast preparations at a counter separating the two rooms. Carolyn happily helps guests plan their itineraries as she prepares the morning fare. Guests make their breakfast selections each evening from a menu of juices, breads, several egg varieties, cinnamon French toast, breakfast meats, and cereals. We found this to be a nice way to make our breakfast more efficient and relaxed.

Located in the Pemigewasset River Valley just south of the White Mountains and convenient to a major highway serving the north country, Colonel Spencer Inn offers easy access to a plethora of sites and activities. Scenic drives through White Mountain National Forest and its many attractions can begin within a few miles of the inn. Major skiing destinations are very close by and a full range of outdoor activities are available year round. There's a pond just across the road for ice skating and the Hills maintain a twenty-two foot sailboat on nearby Newfound Lake which they make available to guests. Mirror Lake and Squam Lake are also nearby and offer public beach access. In early Spring, you may want to visit Colonel Spencer during sugaring season. The Hills make maple syrup just down the road from the inn and guests are welcome to observe the proceedings.

Your family will be comfortable here in any season and the Hills will make your stay an enjoyable one.

Accommodations: Six guest rooms plus a two-room efficiency suite, all with private baths. Cribs, roll-aways, and high chairs available.

Rates: $45-$65, double occupancy, B&B. Children free in room with parents. EP rates are $5 less per person and discounts are available for multiple night stays and during mid-week in off season.

Methods of Payment: Cash, personal check, traveler's check.

Dates of Operation: Open all year.

Children: Appropriate for all ages.

Activities/Facilities: Ice skating, swimming, lake access and sailboat available to guests. White Mountains National Forest, Pemigewasset River, several lakes, full range of winter activities including major ski resorts located nearby.

Rockhouse
Mountain Farm Inn

Innkeepers: Johnny and Alana Edge
Telephone: (603) 447-2880
Address: Eaton Center, NH 03832

If you're looking for a total escape for your family vacation, consider Rockhouse Mountain Farm Inn. Johnny Edge and his family skillfully provide their guests with an authentic and unforget-
table New England farm experience. Nestled in the rolling
foothills of the White Mountains on 450 acres of lush farmland,
the inn provides a warm and very casual retreat for children,
parents, and grandparents. No hint of big city haughtiness or
suburban hustle is evident in the area surrounding the farm.
Eaton Center is not much more than a bend in the road with a
few tidy old buildings and the commensurate little white
church. Johnny and his family and staff prefer to think of the
experience they provide as a "farm vacation" rather than a typical country inn getaway. The collection of buildings at
Rockhouse includes a turn of the century white farmhouse, the

Carriage House, and the Twenty House all with guest accommodations. Flower gardens, scattered lawn furniture, sweeping lawns, large hardwood trees, and vistas of the surrounding valley complete the pastoral setting.

Keeping the kids occupied around here is no problem. This is a working farm and children are welcome in all the daily chores. Morning cow milking is a particular source of excitement. Chickens, cats, peacocks, and a changing variety of semi-domesticated visitors also provide lots of fun (and some education!). During our visit, Johnny was nursing a raven back to health after it suffered a broken wing. He's also built a protective fenced area which is used by Canadian geese and Mallards for their annual breeding. All of this animal life combines with the bucolic country environment and the wonderful, homey perspective of Johnny and his staff to produce a great example of life in a simpler time.

The food is equally authentic. At breakfast time, guests are welcome to stroll out to the chicken coop to collect their morning fare. A cornucopia of accompaniments including fruits, flapjacks, potatoes, juices, coffee, and raw milk (of course) round out the typical menu. Dinners can include an outdoor steak grill or chicken roast and are served outdoors or indoors depending on the weather and Johnny's last minute executive preference. Virtually everything is homemade. From cakes and pies and breads, to the beef, chicken, and milk, the food you consume is a product of the farm and the busy cooks in the kitchen. It provides nourishment for the spirit as well as the body. The dining room is a hodgepodge of tables and chairs. They are arranged however is most appropriate for the occasion. Sometimes children eat in one room and entertain themselves while the adults dine more graciously in the adjoining room. It is common for children to rush through breakfast in the morning so they can get back outside to cavort with each other and the animals, giving parents the luxury of quiet conversation over a second cup of coffee.

The guest rooms offer a mix of shared baths, private baths, and family suites. All are unpretentious and comfortable. There is also a bunkhouse. It is available to any children who want to share it. The flexible, easygoing atmosphere made us feel like we were at a big old-fashioned family reunion.

And we can't forget the beach. Eaton Center sits on the pristine shores of Crystal Lake, a relatively small lake by New Hampshire standards but pretty and very clean. Rockhouse guests have access to their own private beach less than a mile from the inn. It is stocked with everything you need for summertime fun. Canoes, paddle boats, picnic tables, a float dock, and even a swingset anchored in the shallow water make for endless family fun. Your visit to Rockhouse Mountain Farm Inn is sure to produce lots of happy family memories.

Accommodations: 15 rooms plus 3 rooms in the bunkhouse. Some private baths, some shared. Cribs and high chairs available.

Rates: $50-$58, per person, double occupancy, MAP. Reduced rates for children depending on their age when rooming with parents. Typically, guests book for one week stays from Saturday to Saturday.

Methods of Payment: Cash, traveler's check, personal check.

Dates of Operation: Mid-June through October.

Children: Very appropriate for all ages.

Activities/Facilities: Rockhouse is a total experience, with plenty of interest and activities for all ages. All of the scenic areas of the White Mountains and the Maine coast are within an easy day's drive. Weekly picnics at nearby Swift River, outdoor barbecues, hiking, swimming, farm activities.

Kluges' Sunset Hill Inn

Innkeepers: John and Debby Kluge, Sylvia and David Dow
Telephone: (603) 632-4335
Address: Mascoma Lake
*   Enfield, NH 03748*

The Kluge family has been taking guests at this beautifully situated former shaker farm for almost fifty years. A large portion of their summer visitors have been reserving vacation time at the inn for years. If your family is looking for a place to get away from it all and truly relax, then we recommend that you give Kluges' Sunset Hill Inn a call. John and Erna Kluge bought the inn in 1953 and it is now operated by their children, John and Sylvia, who live on the property with their families.

Surrounded by over 300 acres of forests and fields, it truly is an escape from the hectic pace of everyday life. The inn's main building was built in the early 1800's by Shakers who had developed a community on the shores of Lake Mascoma. Until the 1940's, it was a working farm which produced wool, pork, and beef. Wide lawns surround the property and beautiful views are available from almost anywhere. There is plenty of room for children to romp. The Kluges' keep a collection of outdoor toys for their guests. The inground pool is a perfect place to hang out for the afternoon while you soak in the warm sun and breathe the invigorating, pine-scented mountain air. Picnic tables and barbecue grills are also available. A small network of trails meanders through the surrounding woods where wild blueberries and raspberries are abundant. And if all this isn't enough, you can take a short trip down the hill to the private sandy beach at the beach house on Lake Mascoma. A collection of equipment including paddle boats, sunfish sail boats, flotation toys, Adirondack chairs, and canoes awaits your enjoyment. An entertainment room in the main building features cable television with VCR and a collection of movies, pool and ping pong tables, and plenty of games and books.

Five bed and breakfast rooms are located in the main building. Each of these has a private bath and simple comfortable furnishings. There are also several housekeeping suites in buildings bordering the lawn areas. Ranging in size from one to three bedrooms, and including full kitchens, living rooms, and one or two baths, they can comfortably accommodate families of any size.

The dining room is a large, sunny space in the main building. A hearty breakfast is served daily to B&B and housekeeping guests. German pancakes are the specialty of the house or you may choose to start your day with a huge cheese and mushroom omelette or French toast. Fresh fruit, blueberry muffins, cereals, juices, and coffee and tea complement the entrees.

Catering to families has been a focus for the Kluges for decades and it shows in the friendly, enjoyable getaway they have created. Your family will feel welcome here and you may just want to make reservations for next year before you leave.

Accommodations: 5 guest rooms in main house, all with private baths. 8 to 10 housekeeping units with one to three bedrooms, living rooms, full kitchens, and one or two baths. 3 bedroom cottage on Mascoma Lake.

Rates: B&B rooms are $60, double occupancy. Children in cribs are free, $10 for additional persons. Housekeeping suites range from $60 to $90 per night, and $390 to $470 per week. Four night minimum reservation requested. Breakfast for housekeeping guests available for $5, adults and $2.50, children.

Methods of Payment: Cash, personal check, traveler's check.

Dates of Operation: Memorial Day through foliage season.

Children: Appropriate for all ages.

Activities/Facilities: Hiking trails, swimming pool, barbecue grills, recreation room, lakefront beach available on premises. A multitude of historic, entertainment, cultural, and outdoor activities in the immediate area. Lake Mascoma Shaker village offers daily tours, exhibits, and herb gardens in season.

Moose Mountain Lodge

Innkeepers: Kay and Peter Shumway
Telephone: (603) 643-3529
Address: P.O. Box 272
*   Etna, NH 03750*

Communing with nature is a way of life at Moose Mountain Lodge. The inn is located up on a hillside along the western edge of the White Mountains, seven miles east of Hanover, New Hampshire and the Connecticut River. Over 350 surrounding acres of meadows and woodlands provide guests with ample opportunity to experience the pastoral beauty of an unspoiled natural setting. Kay and Peter Shumway have owned and operated Moose Mountain since 1975 and share their guests' enthusiasm for the outdoors.

Popular summertime activities include biking, canoeing, and hiking. There is a preponderance of winding backroads in the area which makes for great bicycle touring and the inn attracts a good number of bicycling groups. The nearby Connecticut River is a favorite with canoeists. Miles of hiking trails traverse the property and adjacent hills. The Appalachian Trail is one of them, affording avid hikers access to an impressive variety of itineraries. Nordic skiing is the prime attraction in winter. Kay and Peter are enthusiastic skiers and often join their guests for tours around the mountain. Tulla, the resident canine, is an accomplished trail guide and is in high demand by guests. The resident staff is also available to lead groups around the extensive network of trails. Ice skating on a seven acre beaver pond is another popular wintertime activity.

The inn's interior is warm, rustic, and comfortable. A large common room is furnished with big couches arranged around a beautiful fireplace. Lots of books are available for quiet evenings and there's also an assortment of games and puzzles. Older children can entertain themselves with the electric keyboard. It has earphones so any racket is nicely contained. The dining room is large and airy. It is a friendly gathering place at any hour. Cookies, coffee, tea, fruit, and other refreshments are always available. The Shumways operate their kitchen with an open concept. Guests are welcome to stop by and chat with the staff, or store personal items in the refrigerator. Children can help with the daily baking and cooking activities.

A beautiful wooden deck is located on the building's west side. It offers wonderful views down to the Connecticut River and across to the Green Mountains of Vermont as far as Killington and Pico ski areas. The kids will enjoy the downstairs recreation room which is a great place for them to spend any leftover energy and not disturb those who want peace and quiet. There's lots of room to roam and the player piano is a favorite of the younger set.

Twelve guest rooms share five sparkling clean baths and offer guests cozy and rustic lodge-style accommodations. Each room features timber frame beds handmade by Kay. One room has a queen bed plus two bunk beds and is called the "Wall to Wall People" room. There's also a room with four bunk beds which is a nice place for kids. Since the inn charges by the person, rather than by the room, a variety of room arrangements are available for families. Kay and Peter try to arrange for several families to reserve for the same days so that more of a family friendly atmosphere can be provided. New found friends are welcome to share the bunk room while parents can enjoy a private night's rest.

Meals at Moose Mountain are appropriately hearty. Guests enjoy a full breakfast before attacking a busy day outdoors. Dinners include a featured entree and a vegetarian alternative, plus a choice of homemade desserts. Snackers are always welcome in the kitchen where there seems to be something good and fresh from the oven almost any time.

There's no television and no stereo at Moose Mountain, which adds to the peaceful and rejuvenating experience the Shumways provide. If your family enjoys nature, you will return regularly to this friendly mountain hideaway.

Accommodations: 12 rooms with shared baths. Crib available.

Rates: Summer and Fall; $80, per person, double occupancy, MAP. Children 12 years and under, $42. Winter; $85, per person, double occupancy, AP. Children 5 years and under, $25. Ages 6-14, $50.

Methods of Payment: Cash, traveler's check, personal check, MasterCard, Visa.

Dates of Operation: December 26 to March 20 and June 1 to October 20.

Children: Not appropriate for infants and toddlers.

Activities/Facilities: 350 acres of mountainside splendor. Hiking, biking, canoeing in summer. Several small farm animals for children to enjoy. Seven acre beaver pond. Nordic skiing haven in winter. Close to Dartmouth College and other activities in Hanover, NH and nearby Vermont.

Fitzwilliam Inn

Innkeepers: The Wallace Family
Telephone: (603) 585-9000
Address: RR1, Box 27
*   Fitzwilliam, NH 03447-9607*

Fitzwilliam Inn has been serving weary travelers since 1796. Today it retains the easy-going country atmosphere that earlier visitors enjoyed. Set ever so perfectly on the Fitzwilliam town green, the inn is immediately reminiscent of colonial New England.

The guest rooms and common areas are simply decorated and present clean, functional, and charming environs. Comfortable furnishings are arranged in cozy fashion on an assortment of area and room-sized rugs with just the right amount of sway in the wooden floors underneath. Guest rooms are located on the second and third floors. About half the rooms have private baths. Many rooms have multiple beds and several have fireplaces. We really felt comfortable here. The Wallaces and their staff were very welcoming and more than willing to help us in any way.

The inn's main floor contains an array of common areas and the popular restaurant and pub. The european plan pricing for guest rooms allows you to take whichever meals you desire at the restaurant. The dining room features a fireplace, exposed beams, and hand-painted stenciling. Simple wooden tables and chairs are cozily arranged to provide a charming atmosphere. Patio seating is also available in a more secluded adjoining room. The pub is a great place to enjoy a favorite beverage at the end of your daily adventures or after dinner. Wooden bench seats, an imposing brick fireplace, a well-worn bar, and pine-paneled walls make the pub a comfortable refuge. The parlor room features a grand piano, empire sofas, and another fireplace. The Wallaces host a Sunday afternoon winter concert series here. A small alcove across the hall is reserved for a quaint gift shop. Local crafts, pure maple syrup, and Fitzwilliam Inn memorabilia are the primary offerings. Finally, the library contains a game table, a television and VCR, and shelves full of books, games, puzzles, and magazines.

The dinner menu offers about a dozen entees which all sounded wonderful. Fresh venison with brandied cajun peppercorn sauce is a local favorite and was absolutely delicious. Other items include fresh swordfish and trout, broiled pork chops with cranberry orange sauce, veal chops with sherried mushrooms and eggplant Baton Rouge with florentine tortellini. Complete dinners are reasonably priced and include soup, salad, bread, coffee or tea, and one of Barbara Wallace's famous homemade desserts. Her coconut cream pie is fabulous.

There are plenty of local events, activities, and sites to take in on your visit to Fitzwilliam. The village itself begs to be strolled through in any season. Beautifully maintained antique buildings encircle the green and line the adjacent tributary streets. Mount

Monadnock is a very short drive away. This popular hiking and picnic spot offers numerous trails to the summit. On a clear day, the view from the top can include parts of five states. Antiquing is very popular in the area. The Wallaces regularly direct guests to the best little shops in the region. Cultural events and local town fairs are abundant all summer long. And lest we forget, occasional murder mystery events and the aforementioned winter concerts are offered right at the inn. There is also an outdoor pool for summer frolicking and cross-country skiing on five miles of groomed trails in the winter. Sleigh rides, hay rides, orchards, petting farms, and golf are all available in season nearby.

Accommodations: 28 guest rooms, most with private baths. Rollaways and cribs available.

Rates: $35-$55, double occupancy, EP. $10 for extra persons. $3 for cribs.

Methods of Payment: Cash, traveler's check, personal check, major credit cards.

Dates of Operation: Open all year.

Children: Appropriate for all ages, though best suited for children of grade school age and older.

Activities/Facilities: Game room, outdoor swimming pool, conference facilities, lounge, restaurant, gift shop on premises. Antique shops, hiking, skiing, golf, historical sites, cultural events in the immediate vicinity.

The Inn at Crotched Mountain

Innkeepers: John and Rose Perry
Telephone: (603) 588-6840
Address: Mountain Road
Francestown, NH 03043

John and Rose Perry refer to The Inn at Crotched Mountain as "an out of the way inn". It is also out of this world. The panoramic view from this mountainside retreat stretches out over forty miles of the beautiful Piscataquog Valley. The inn is located on sixty acres of former farm land on the northern side of Crotched Mountain in New Hampshire's picturesque Monadnock region. John and Rose combine warm hospitality with their hearty, home cooked meals and a plethora of outdoor activities to create a truly wonderful family experience.

Summertime activities include swimming in the inn's huge outdoor pool. There is also a wading pool for the tots and a lifeguard is on duty all summer long. Two beautiful clay tennis courts are also available for guests. Mountainside hikes are practically a must in this serene country environment. Bring your fishing pole along for a quiet afternoon of angling in the numerous streams, ponds, and lakes. The huge lawn behind the inn is great for lawn games and romping with children. Some guests even bring baseballs and gloves for impromptu ballgames during their stay. Plenty of golfing, antique shopping, and historical sites are located nearby. Wintertime activities include downhill skiing at two nearby areas and Nordic skiing on miles of trails on the inn's property.

The 150 year old structure was partially burned down in the 1930's and was rebuilt with an interest in maintaining its original style. Thirteen guest rooms offer clean and comfortable accommodations. Lots of windows create a bright, airy feel and there are not a lot of delicate or breakable furnishings. Many rooms feature private fireplaces. Several rooms have multiple beds and adjoining rooms with a shared bath work well for families. One main floor guest room also has a private entrance. The "Penthouse" suite is located on the second floor and has two bedrooms and a full bath. Several quaint common rooms offer visitors plenty of relaxation and convivial conversation. A nightcap in the twin-hearthed living room is particularly pleasurable.

The Perrys are both formally educated in hotel and restaurant management and they have operated the inn since 1976. Their education and experience is evident throughout the inn, but probably most of all in the dining room. Rose is the chef and she specializes in savory, home style dinners that appeal to the traditional palate such as roast pork, sirloin steak, and stuffed chicken breast. The prompt and attentive service makes dining pleasurable even for families with young children.

The Inn at Crotched Mountain combines a beautiful countryside setting with warm, hospitable service that your entire family will enjoy.

Accommodations: 13 guest rooms, 8 with private bath, 5 with shared bath. Roll-aways and high chairs available.

Rates: $70-$100, double occupancy, B&B. $20 for extra person in same room. $120-$160, double occupancy, MAP. $40 for extra person in same room.

Methods of Payment: Cash, traveler's check, personal check.

Dates of Operation: Open all year except April and November.

Children: Appropriate for all ages.

Activities/Facilities: Swimming, tennis, hiking, yard games, fishing, Nordic skiing available on premises. Golf, antiquing, historical sites, down hill skiing in immediate vicinity.

The Franconia Inn

Innkeepers: Richard and Alec Morris
Telephone: (603) 823-5542
Address: Route 116
*   Easton Road*
*   Franconia, NH 03580*

Richard and Alec Morris represent the Morris family's third gen-
eration of innkeepers. The depth of their experience and their
commitment to providing enjoyable family vacations is very
much in evidence at The Franconia Inn. The inn is located in the
beautiful Easton Valley and is surrounded by the towering
peaks of the Franconia and Kinsman ranges of the White
Mountains. Awe inspiring views of Mount Lafayette and
Franconia Notch add to the splendor of this beautiful country
getaway. The inn was originally built in 1868 and was completely rebuilt after a fire in 1934. The large three story building
retains its nineteenth century charm with white clapboard siding, shuttered windows, multiple chimneys, and wide porches.
There are over 100 acres of beautiful countryside to explore.

The wide range of family activities available on the inn's property will keep even the most enthusiastic families busy for days. Of particular note is the glider port within 100 yards of the inn's front door. Novices and experienced fliers can sign up for a fantastic aerial tour of the surrounding mountains and valleys during summer months. Fall foliage viewing is a spectacular experience from the seat of a gently soaring glider. Equestrian pursuits are also available at the inn's own stable. Horseback riding and hay rides can be arranged during summer months and sleigh rides complete with jingling bells are popular in winter. The barn building also serves as a cross-country ski touring center complete with equipment rentals and instruction. There are miles of meadow and forest trails for horseback riders and hikers in the summertime and cross-country skiers in the winter. Four clay tennis courts and a heated outdoor swimming pool are available, and badminton and croquet equipment can be checked out at the front desk. Tandem and single bicycles, some even with kiddie seats, can be rented for a healthy tour of Easton Valley. For the naturalist, a cool, clear swimming hole is located a short distance from the inn. Ice skates and sleds can be rented for brisk winter activity for the whole family.

Visitors can enjoy a number of indoor activities and functions after a refreshing day spent outdoors. Family movies are shown every evening and a recreation room in the basement provides plenty of fun for the children. A family-sized hot tub is a popular attraction for those with sore muscles from the day's activities. Parents might enjoy a quiet drink in the Rathskellar Lounge after the children retire. Baby monitors are available upon request.

The dining room is casually elegant with linen tablecloths and candlelight. Children's menus are available for the kids and babysitting services can be arranged so parents can enjoy a more romantic dining experience.

The Franconia Inn has thirty-four guest rooms with a number of comfortable family arrangements available. Several rooms contain double or queen beds and a twin bed and two family suites can comfortably accommodate a family of six. This inn is great for weekend getaways or extended family vacations and once you enjoy your first visit, you will probably want to return again and again.

Accommodations: 34 guest rooms, all with private baths. High chairs, booster seats, and roll-aways available.

Rates: $58-$113, double occupancy, EP. $125-$180, double occupancy, MAP. Children under 6 years, no charge. Ages 6 to 11, $5, EP, and $21.25, MAP. B&B rates and numerous discount packages available.

Methods of Payment: Cash, traveler's check, personal check, MasterCard, Visa, American Express.

Dates of Operation: Open all year except April.

Children: Appropriate for all ages.

Activities/Facilities: Hiking, swimming, biking, tennis, soaring, horseback riding, lawn games in summer. Nordic skiing, ice skating, sledding, sleigh rides in winter. Video games, movies, library, hot tub, and lounge. Golf, downhill skiing, antiquing, numerous family attractions available nearby.

The Greenfield Inn

Innkeepers: Barbara and Vic Mangini
Address: Route 31, Box 400
*   Forest Road*
*   Greenfield, NH 03040*
Telephone: (603) 547-6327 (800) 678-4144

Greenfield, New Hampshire is just the kind of place you would expect to see if you stepped into a typical Currier and Ives painting. White picket fences, pastoral farms, and classic New England architecture give the town the whimsical feel of a bygone era. This is a less traveled part of the state and the pace of life is refreshingly slow and easy. Barbara and Vic Mangini have added to the local ambiance with the establishment of The Greenfield Inn. Beautifully set just off one of Greenfield's main streets, the inn greets travelers with a wide country porch, abundant flower gardens, and a beautiful 3-acre lawn. White clapboard siding and lots of shuttered windows give this 175 year old building a friendly warmth.

Barbara's decorating style is evident throughout the house. Every room is filled with lots of comfortable furniture and an abundance of artwork, decorative tables, and Victorian style lamps and accessories. Three common rooms are located on the ground floor. A cozy living room at the front of the house is a nice place to mingle with other guests, watch a movie on the VCR, or read a favorite book from the Manginis' large selection. The White Wicker Garden Room is located adjacent to the dining room and overlooks the large lawn area to the west of the building. There's a supply of board games and a basket of dolls and toys for guests to enjoy. The dining room is large and comfortable. The huge dining table can easily accommodate a houseful of visitors. Crystal decanters of sherry and dishes filled with candies are liberally set out around the house as a constant treat for guests.

Most of the inn's nine guest rooms are located on the second floor. Five rooms with private baths and three with shared baths are available in addition to the huge Hayloft suite with private bath and kitchenette. Several rooms have multiple beds and two rooms with their shared bath can be made into a family suite. A few rooms have televisions, air-conditioning, and telephones. Victorian charm is evident throughout the inn's guest rooms. Sheets, bedspreads, table cloths, towels, and window coverings share a bright, coordinated pattern that gives each room a warm, cheery feel.

Barbara provides a hearty, buffet-style breakfast each morning consisting of egg casseroles, souffles, homemade muffins, and a variety of cereals, juices, and coffee. And there's plenty of family activities in the area to take in after breakfast. Hiking at Mount Monadnock, skiing at Temple and Crotched Mountains, and swimming, picnicking, and boating at Greenfield State Park are all within minutes of the inn. A wealth of antique shops are in the vicinity and a nice long walk around the quaint village is a joy. There is also a children's museum and a small animal farm nearby.

Barbara and Vic are warm and outgoing and pride themselves in providing friendly, personalized service. Your family will enjoy a visit to this lovely country getaway.

Accommodations: 9 guest rooms including hayloft suite which sleeps 6. Roll-aways available.

Rates: $49-$99, double occupancy, B&B. Hayloft suite is $99, double occupancy, EP, plus $20 for each additional person. Weekly rates available.

Methods of Payment: Cash, traveler's check, personal check. Visa and MasterCard accepted.

Dates of Operation: Open all year.

Children: Not appropriate for infants or toddlers.

Activities/Facilities: Hiking, swimming, boating, and scenic drives. Golfing, skiing, hay and sleigh rides, children's museum, antique shopping nearby.

Stillmeadow
Bed and Breakfast

Innkeepers:Lori and Randy Offord
Telephone: (603) 329-8381
Address: P.O. Box 565
*   Hampstead, NH 03841*

Here's a small bed and breakfast that has all the charm and
warmth that originally made this type of lodging so popular.
The building itself is a wonderful example of Italianate Greek
Renaissance architecture with carved eave supports, fancy window trim, and plenty of windows. The Offords have landscaped
the three acre property to embellish this beautiful structure.
Formal hedges, flowering shrubs, stone walls, and brick walk-
ways surround the grounds. The house, built in the 1850's, features five chimneys, three staircases, and sixty-five windows.
Common rooms consist of a comfortable sitting room, well-
appointed dining room, and a great playroom for youngsters
under caring parental supervision. The playroom has a varied
collection of toys, cable television with a VCR, and plenty of

space to stretch out. It is also the most likely place to find your hosts and their two children, Ashleigh and Benjamin.

Four guest rooms are located on the second floor. They range in size from a cozy single room to the Tulip Suite, which is the best room for families. It features two queen beds plus a daybed which converts to a crib. It includes a huge bathroom with changing table and double sinks as well as a private television and refrigerator. All of the rooms are decorated with beautiful wallpaper, country curtains, and classic period furnishings. The inn's interior matches the exterior in crispness and eye appeal.

Lori and Randy Offord are wonderful hosts. They are always available for dining and entertainment references or warm conversation. The cookie jar is always full and the Offords even provide complimentary wine for all their guests upon arrival. Breakfast is continental style and includes homemade muffins and breads, fruit, cereal, and yogurt. Guests are invited to relax on the country porch, stroll the lawns and gardens, or play with the children in the play yard. Lori can also provide babysitting references for guests staying in the Tulip Suite.

Stillmeadow is located within easy driving distance to New Hampshire's seacoast, mountains, and lakes regions as well as the Boston, Portsmouth, and Manchester metropolitan areas. It would make a great place to visit with your family when you are in the area for business or pleasure.

Accommodations: 4 guest rooms, all with private bath.

Rates: $50-$95, double occupancy, B&B.

Methods of Payment: Cash, traveler's check, personal check, American Express, MasterCard, and Visa.

Dates of Operation: Open all year.

Children: Appropriate for all ages.

Activities/Facilities: Convenient access to Boston and a variety of coastal and country activities. Amusement park and working dairy farm tours nearby.

The Inn at Elmwood Corners

Innkeepers: John and Mary Hornberger
Telephone: (603) 929-0443, (800) 253-5691
Address: 252 Winnacunnet Road
*   Hampton, NH 03842*

The Inn at Elmwood Corners is a great little place for a family getaway if you want to spend some time at the beach but prefer to avoid the often cramped and noisy accommodations available at the water's edge. Located less than two miles from the water, the inn offers clean, nicely decorated rooms and plenty of space to stretch out and relax after a busy day. Some of New Hampshire's most popular beaches, including Hampton, Jenness, and Rye Harbor, are only minutes away.

Plenty of diverse activities in the area make this a good place to escape to in any season. The town of Hampton is quaint and offers a number of good family restaurants as well as movie theatres, the Hampton Playhouse, and shopping at the Hampton Village shops. Historic Portsmouth is just up the road. Your family might enjoy a visit to Strawbery Banke, a completely restored seventeenth century village and museum in the heart of Portsmouth. Outlet shopping at Kittery, Maine is within fifteen miles. Newburyport, Massachusetts is also within fifteen miles and is a great place to spend a day shopping, taking in the scenic harbor, and enjoying the day's catch at any number of local restaurants. When you return from your day's activities, John and Mary Hornberger will welcome you with their relaxed, unpretentious style and warm hospitality. The inn offers seven guest rooms including two studio rooms with multiple beds, private baths, and kitchenettes. The other five rooms share three baths and several have room enough for roll-away beds or cribs. Each room has a different floral or color theme and features Mary's own stenciling and handmade quilts which are really beautiful. Her handiwork is also evident in the hand woven baskets sprinkled throughout the house. The Hornbergers have done a lot of renovating in this 125 year old building and it now has all the modern conveniences while retaining its original charm. There are some well done exposed beams and John has a before and after photo album which is really interesting for those who tinker with restoration.

Guests can enjoy several common rooms and a spacious yard. The parlor has easy chairs and a television and is across the hall from the library room, where books, games, and puzzles can be found. The dining room has an entire wall of windows overlooking the gardens and lawn. John does all the cooking and many of his dishes feature seasonal fruits and produce from his own garden or nearby farms. Guests can choose from two or three daily breakfast entrees including one non-egg dish and a low cholesterol option. The Hornbergers also offer dinner for guests on a pre-arranged basis. Dining in is often an attractive option for families tired of restaurant meals.

The front of the building is enwrapped by a wide, covered porch with wicker furniture and lots of flower pots. The yard area is primarily located on the side and to the rear of the inn. It offers plenty of room to roam and nicely tended bushes and flower gardens. There is also an abundance of wild tiger lilies popping up all over the yard in Summer.

A brick barbecue grill is available for guest use along with a couple of picnic tables. The Hornbergers have two sons, Keith and Kevin 6 who are more than happy to take visiting children on a tour of the property.

John and Mary have lots of information about local attractions and willingly assist guests in designing their daily itineraries. We enjoyed our visit and think your family will, too.

Accommodations: 5 guest rooms, sharing 3 baths, and 2 suites with private baths. Roll-aways available.

Rates: $65-$75, double occupancy, B&B. Suites are $75-$85, B&B. Extra persons, $10 each.

Methods of Payment: Cash, traveler's check, personal check, MasterCard, Visa.

Dates of Operation: Open all year.

Children: Appropriate for all ages.

Activities/Facilities: Large yard with barbecue grill, picnic tables, gardens, TV, board games, books in common rooms. Area attractions include several beaches, shopping, historic sites, local theatre, scenic drives, family restaurants, water parks, orchards.

Christmas Farm Inn

Innkeepers: Sydna and Bill Zeliff
Telephone: (603) 383-4313, (800) HI ELVES
Address: Route 16B
*   Box CC*
*   Jackson, NH 03846*

North Pole magic can be enjoyed all year long at Christmas Farm Inn. A happy holiday spirit permeates this sprawling mountain inn and its entire staff, who refer to themselves as the "Elves." If you could imagine a "destination resort" of country inns, this would be it. We were overwhelmed by the choice of activities available at the inn, not to mention the wide variety of family attractions in the Jackson area.

Thirty-five guest rooms are available in the main building (a 1786 farm house), the neighboring Salt Box building (circa 1778), suites in the Barn building, and several cottages spread over the surrounding hillside. There are lots of great arrangements for families. The barn suites include color TV and telephones and lots of room for the whole family. Downstairs, the barn has a large family room serving all four suites. With its huge field-stone fireplace and sauna room, it's a perfect place to unwind and recover from a full day's skiing. It also contains table games, a big screen TV, and a piano. Several two bedroom cottages are also available. These feature sundecks, fireplaces, refrigerators, telephones, and TV's. The main inn and saltbox rooms are less appropriate for small children, but fine for families with teenagers staying in separate rooms. The rooms are beautifully decorated with classic furniture, country wall coverings, and modern baths.

The primary common rooms are located in the main inn. The roomy parlor is a great gathering spot. Guests enjoy casual conversation, games, and a TV with a VCR for movies. A cozy fireplace and re-stored wide-pine floors create a warm and hospitable air. There's also an adjoining sitting room for reading or other quieter activities. Tucked away in a small room behind the front desk is the Mistletoe Pub, a great place for parents to enjoy a nightcap after the children are asleep.

Dining is a pleasurable experience at the Christmas Farm. We found the dining room ambiance to be pleasant and enjoyable for parents while not being too elegant for children. Your kids will love the pretty Christmas lights which brighten the room all year long. A separate area off to the side of the main dining area can be reserved for larger families or those with small children. High chairs are available and children can color while they wait to be served. Youngsters can order from the Elves menu, stocked with kiddy favorites.

A visit to the Christmas Farm Inn in any season affords guests with countless options for outdoor activities. Summertime is great for golf at local clubs, hiking, fishing, and cycling in the surrounding White Mountains, and a lot of fun on the inn's grounds. How about swimming in a spring-fed outdoor pool, or a game of badminton on the spacious lawn. You can even sharpen your game on the inn's own putting green while the kids enjoy the playground area. Skiing is king in winter. The barn serves as the center of activity for daily outings and guests can enjoy a warm drink by the roaring fire at the end of the day. Nordic skiers can ply their efforts on over 150 kilometers of world famous trails right from the inn's doors. Downhill skiers will enjoy the preponderance of quality slopes in the area. For the less adventurous, loads of great outlet stores and shops in the area provide a wealth of tax free opportunities. Simply stated, you can find plenty to do no matter what your interests are.

Accommodations: 35 guest rooms, all with private baths, (five with jacuzzis), including suites and private cottages for families. Roll-aways and cribs available.

Rates: $68-$95 per person, double occupancy, MAP. Children under 12 in room with parents, $25, MAP. Numerous package plans available for 3 day weekends, mid-week stays, etc.

Methods of Payment: Cash, traveler's check, personal check, American Express, MasterCard, and Visa accepted.

Dates of Operation: Open all year.

Children: Appropriate for all ages.

Activities/Facilities: Swimming, hiking, biking, golf, tennis, shopping, theme parks, horseback riding, canoeing, etc. available in summer. Lots of skiing and a full range of winter sports activities in season. Games, books, fine dining at the inn. Pool, table tennis, lounge and TV's with VCR's and a selection of movies. Many rooms have private TV's, some also have jacuzzis.

The Inn at Jackson

Innkeeper: *Lori Tradewell*
Telephone: *(603) 383-4321, (800) 289-8600*
Address: *P.O. Box 807*
Jackson, NH 03846

Spacious, comfortable accommodations and casual, friendly hospitality are the hallmarks of The Inn at Jackson. Innkeeper Lori Tradewell is merrily assisted by her bright-eyed young daughter, Rachel. They provide a warm welcome to weary travelers and promote the cozy atmosphere which prevails at this White Mountain getaway. With over eight years in residence at the inn, Lori is adept at guiding guests to their favorite country activity.

The Inn at Jackson is a large, old, gambrel-roofed building which sits on a small rise overlooking the scenic mountain village of Jackson. Its brick red exterior and white trim matches the covered bridge just down the road at the entrance to the village. Inside, the rooms and common areas are large, airy, and very clean. The main entry hall is two stories high and very wide with a beautiful open staircase against a wall of windows at the back. It's a bright and cheery room which adds to the convivial atmosphere at the inn. Eight guest rooms are located upstairs. Each is large and comfortable with country wallpaper, wood floors, white wooden trim work, and big windows. We were able to comfortably fit a roll-away bed in our room. Large full baths are located in each room, and three rooms have fireplaces.

There are three large common rooms in addition to the main entry hall where Lori, Rachel, and their guests gather for games, movies, and conversation. Tucked away upstairs is a smaller common room with a TV and casual furnishings. It's a great place for kids to hang out while their parents are entertaining themselves downstairs. Guests also gather in a large sitting area at the top of the stairs which accesses all the guest rooms. Magazines, books, and brochures for local attractions are here for your perusal. Finally, there is a parlor on the main floor where most guests tend to gather. Games and puzzles, a TV, and a beautiful fireplace provide great entertainment after a day in the outdoors. Rachel has lots of toys and games that she is anxious to share with new found friends.

Breakfast is served in a pretty and informal dining room with another fireplace and also on the screened porch in warmer months. Lori offers her guests several entree choices including a variety of eggs, breakfast meats, and hotcakes (we loved the blueberry pancakes). Coffees, teas, juices, and hot cocoa, along with muffins, fresh fruits, and a variety of cold cereals round out the fare.

The Mount Washington Valley offers a plenitude of family activities. Summertime attractions include hiking, biking, golf, swimming, fishing, hay rides, and several theme parks in the surrounding area. Wintertime activities center around cross-country skiing right from the inn on over 150 kilometers of trails maintained by the Jackson Ski Touring Foundation, and down-hill skiing at four nearby resorts. There's also ice skating, horse-drawn sleigh rides, and lots of craft and outlet stores in the area. Lori is well versed on local activities and events and is always at the ready to assist her guests in planning their outings.

Accommodations: 12 rooms, all with private baths. Roll-away beds and booster chairs available.

Rates: $59-$129, double occupancy, B&B.

Methods of Payment: Cash, traveler's check, personal check, MasterCard, Visa, American Express.

Dates of Operation: Open all year.

Children: Appropriate for all ages.

Activities/Facilities: Games, puzzles, TV's, books, and some children's toys available at the inn. There is also an outdoor jacuzzi. Full range of year-round outdoor activities available in the immediate area.

Whitneys' Inn Jackson

Innkeepers:Kevin Martin
Telephone: (603) 383-8916, (800) 677-5737
Address: Route 16B
            P.O. Box 822
            Jackson, NH 03846-0822

Here's a place that's great for families looking for lots of organized activities designed for both children and adults. Although
this is not exclusively a getaway for families, we were impressed
with the wide range of family oriented activities available.

Children will enjoy the supervised morning activities program
offered two days each week. Right after breakfast, kids gather in
the lower level of the inn's Shovel Handle Pub for three hours of
fun and games (no parents allowed!). Each day's activities are
based on the ages, interests, and abilities of the children in atten-
dance. A typical morning might include swimming, crafts, outdoor games, hikes, movies, or whatever interests the children.
Snacks and drinks are provided. A children's dinner table is also

available each evening except Wednesdays for children old enough to be unsupervised. After the waitstaff provides a healthy full meal, kids can gather in the game room for movies, games, or coloring as they please. Parents can then enjoy a more formal and quiet dining experience while their children occupy themselves. A lobster cookout is held outdoors down by the pond on Wednesday evenings in lieu of dining room service during warm months. It's a great opportunity to meet the parents of all the friends your children have made.

Besides the organized activities, there's no shortage of things to do at Whitneys'. The inn sits at the base of the Black Mountain ski area. Guests can catch the lift right from the back door. Cross-country skiing on a local network of 150 kilometers of trails is also available from the inn. Ice skating on the pond and great sledding hills round out the primary winter activities. For the summer vacationer, Whitneys' offers paddle boats, canoes, and swimming at the pond (there's lots of frogs which fascinated our children). A tennis court, basketball, volleyball, horseshoes, croquet, and shuffleboard are also popular.

The accommodations at Whitneys' are comfortable, clean, and offer many options for the traveling family. Two cottages located next to the inn offer large bedrooms, fireplaced living rooms with hide-a-bed couches, full baths, and a kitchenette area with sink and refrigerator. Televisions can be checked out at the main desk if you want to spend a quiet night in. The Family Suites building offers nine spacious suites each including a bedroom with double and twin beds, living rooms with two more twin beds, full baths, sinks, refrigerators, and a dining table.

Kevin Martin is a warm and gracious host with many years experience at the inn. His staff is friendly, and very helpful. Whitneys' Inn Jackson will make a fine vacation destination for any family.

Accommodations: 30 rooms with private baths and numerous family suites and cottages. Cribs and roll-aways available.

Rates: $52-$83, per person, double occupancy, MAP. Children under 12 years staying with parents, $12-$25. Package plans and B&B rates available. Cottage and Suite rates based on four-person occupancy.

Methods of Payment: Cash, traveler's check, personal check, MasterCard, Visa, American Express.

Dates of Operation: Open all year.

Children: Appropriate for all ages.

Activities/Facilites: Tennis, lawn games, swimming pond with sandy beach, downhill and cross-country skiing, game room with table games, and VCR library available at inn. Shopping, hiking, sightseeing, theme parks available nearby. Cable T.V. and refrigerators in Family Suite and Cottages.

Loch Lyme Lodge

Innkeepers: Paul and Judy Barker
Telephone: (603) 795-2141 (800) 423-2141
Address: RFD 278
*   Route 10*
*   Lyme, NH 03768*

Paul and Judy Barker are carrying on a family tradition of hospitality dating back to 1946 at Loch Lyme Lodge. Their laid back approach and appreciation of traditional family values make a stay at the Loch Lyme a happy and very enjoyable experience. Here is a place that not only welcomes families, but thrives on them. Many guests have returned year after year, and some for several generations, to enjoy a simple and fulfilling family vacation that hasn't changed much as the world has become more complicated and demanding. Children make friends here with whom they renew friendships annually. Some families come at the same time each year and see many of the people they met on previous visits. Judy is even having some difficulty scheduling her own two sons' activities around the visits of their many annual friends.

During the summer, Loch Lyme visitors can take their pick of twenty-four rustic cabins scattered around the forested hillside or can stay in one of four guest rooms in the main house. From Labor Day to Memorial Day only three main house guest rooms are available. Each cabin contains a full, clean bath, a living room, and one or more bedrooms. Some have kitchens, fireplaces, screen porches and other amenities. Furnishings are simple, rustic, and comfortable. You don't have to worry about a little tracked in dirt or a damp bathing suit here. We felt very welcome and the Barkers encouraged us to just be ourselves.

Located on over 100 acres of woodlands, fields, and lakeshore, Loch Lyme offers an endless variety of good, clean, family activities. The property borders Post Pond and offers a full range of water activities. Rowboats, canoes, sailboards, a sandy beach, dockside fishing, and a floating diving raft will keep any family busy on a hot summer day. Lots of toys are also available for the tots, and they are everywhere. There's even a small slide at the water's edge for splash-happy toddlers. Dozens of Adirondack chairs dot the adjacent lawn where parents can relax while their children frolic.

Across from the main building is a large, communal lawn area which has several swingsets and jungle gyms, a badminton/volleyball net, a playhouse, and all kinds of balls, bats, bikes, and scooters. Just up the hill is a huge vegetable garden meticulously maintained by Judy's father. Its produce is happily consumed by hungry guests. There is a basketball court, baseball field, and a soccer goal out behind the barn and two clay tennis courts over by the garden. It is obvious that the Barkers have honed their brand of family hospitality over the course of many years.

The summer staff at Loch Lyme is comprised largely of college students from a variety of European and U.S. homes. We enjoyed mingling with this entourage of vibrant and happy youths. Meals are served at a collection of tables arranged in three rooms in the main building. Waitpersons offer a daily choice of several country style breakfast and dinner entrees and a selection of home baked desserts. There are plenty of high chairs and booster seats available for the little ones, and special kiddy drinks are a popular accompaniment. Picnic lunches and self-serve mid-day ice cream treats are available as well. Sunday dinners are served outdoors at the lake.

Once you experience Loch Lyme Lodge, you just might become another one of the happy families who look forward to an annual visit.

Accommodations: 24 summer season cottages with private baths, and 3 year-round guest rooms with shared bath. Roll-aways, cribs, high chairs, and booster seats available.

Rates: $29-$42, per person, double occupancy, B&B. $45-$56, per person, double occupancy, MAP. No charge for children 4 years and under. Ages 5 to 15 are $15-$25, B&B and $23-$30, MAP. Housekeeping cottages $390-$650 per week. Multiple discounts and package plans available. Additional meals available for a nominal charge. Small crib or roll-away charge may apply.

Methods of Payment: Cash, traveler's check, personal check.

Dates of Operation: Summer cabins available Memorial Day to Labor Day. Main house rooms available all year except Thanksgiving and Christmas Day.

Children: Appropriate for all ages.

Activities/Facilities: Swimming, boating, hiking, fishing, lawn games, basketball, tennis, Nordic skiing and ice skating available on premises. Downhill skiing, shopping, sightseeing, golf in immediate area.

Cranmore Mountain Lodge

Innkeepers: Dennis and Judy Helfand
Telephone: (603) 356-2044, (800) 356-3596
Address: P.O. Box 1194
North Conway, NH 03860

Despite the extensive variety of activities available at Cranmore Mountain Lodge and in the immediate vicinity, we think that Dennis and Judy Helfand might be the main reason so many of their guests are repeat customers. We were struck by their engaging personalities and very friendly demeanor. Innkeeping is a second career "dream" for the Helfands. After a productive career with a major oil company, Dennis took advantage of an early retirement opportunity and the family set out to find the perfect inn to call their own. They found it here in North Conway. Judy and Dennis feel that successful innkeepers inject their own personalities into the operation, and judging by their magnanimous hospitality, they are an unqualified success.

Dennis is a natural host and entertainer. He plays piano and is more than happy to participate in an evening sing-a-long. He is also well versed in the cultures and lifestyles of native Alaska.

A several year stint in the Alaskan wilderness while with the oil company left a lifelong impression on the Helfands. Dennis has an extensive slide show presentation he delivers to local groups and guests by arrangement. He is also the chief animal husband on the property. A collection of ducks, sheep, rabbits, and a cow reside in a small barn out behind the inn's pond. Dennis and Judy have their sheep sheared and make wool blankets and accessories used throughout the inn. Children and adults are welcome to cavort with this menagerie and help with feeding if they like.

There are plenty of other activities to keep you busy during your stay. A forty-foot swimming pool and jacuzzi hot tub are located right outside the back door. A tennis court, volleyball court, and basketball court are also available for guests. The large back yard is a great place for lawn games or a little game of tag with the sheep. The barn building houses a large game room with an imposing fireplace, table tennis, and cable TV with VCR. Kearsarge Brook borders the property and guests can enjoy a brisk walk along an extensive trail network accessible from the back yard. The Helfands frequently host an evening barbecue in the summertime which is a favorite with their regular guests.

Winter sports enthusiasts enjoy downhill skiing at four local areas including Cranmore Mountain, just down the road. A local ski touring association maintains an extensive trail system in the surrounding hills. There's also skating on the pond which is lighted for nighttime use.

The inn offers seventeen guest rooms and four bunk rooms in the adjoining barn building. All the rooms and the entire inn are clean and comfortable. Many of the rooms in the main building have multiple beds and one room can comfortably accommodate a family of six. Room 2 has historical significance. It's where Babe Ruth used to stay when he visited his daughter and son-in-law who ran the inn in the 1940's. John F. Kennedy, Jr. has also been a guest at Cranmore. All rooms in the main building have private baths and one two-bedroom suite with a bath is available. A fully equipped two-bedroom, two-bath townhouse is also available. Four loft suites are located in the barn building. Each of these rooms has a private bath, color TV, and air conditioning. A unique feature of Cranmore Mountain Lodge are the bunk rooms located in the barn building. Each of these four rooms can accommodate from four to thirteen people and they work great for family reunions or group travel.

Accommodations: 16 rooms with private bath. Plus two-bedroom townhouse. Also 4 bunk rooms with shared bath. Roll-aways, cribs, high chairs are available.

Rates: April-October: $59-$145, double occupancy, B&B. Children under 10 in room with parents, $10, B&B. Add $10 per room during foliage season. Bunk rooms $29, per person, B&B. November-March: $100-$180, double occupancy, MAP. Children under 10 in rooms with parents, $20, MAP. Bunk rooms available for groups.

Methods of Payment: Cash, traveler's check, personal check, Visa, MasterCard, American Express, Discover, Diners Club.

Dates of Operation: Open all year.

Children: Appropriate for all ages.

Activities/Facilities: Outdoor swimming pool and hot tub, tennis court, volleyball, basketball, yard games. Farm animals, natural pond, stream frontage. Hiking trails, indoor recreation room, summer cookouts. Alpine and Nordic skiing, ice skating, and fireside pizza parties in winter. Expansive outlet shopping and family attractions in immediate vicinity.

The 1785 Inn

Innkeepers: Rebecca and Charles Mallar
Telephone: (603) 356-9025, Reservations (800) 421-1785
Address: P.O. Box 1785
*   North Conway, NH 03860-1785*

The White Mountains National Forest stretches over 760,000 acres of New Hampshire's richest resources of wildlife, lakes, streams, mountains, and good old-fashioned New England hospitality. The 1785 Inn is located alongside the "Scenic Vista" on Route 16 sharing its spectacular view of Mount Washington, the premier landmark of the White Mountains National Forest. The inn was built in 1785 by Elijah Dinsmore, a veteran of the French and Indian Wars and the American Revolution. One of the oldest houses in the region, the inn reflects late eighteenth century charm and architecture including the original central chimney with its three fireplaces and brick beehive oven, hand-hewn beams, and exposed corner posts. Six acres of sprawling lawns and flower gardens surround the inn.

Innkeepers Becky and Charlie Mallar along with there three teen-aged daughters provide a wonderful atmosphere for families. Three common rooms and two dining rooms are found on the first floor of the inn. The living room houses a television and VCR as well as numerous board games, books, puzzles, and a good selection of family videos. A pint-size rocking chair along with other comfortable furnishings make this the most frequented common room at the inn. The inn's lounge is casual yet handsome with its woodburning stove, large well-worn bar, and inviting sofas and chairs to relax in and enjoy your favorite beverage and conversation. The inn's dining rooms also enjoy views of Mount Washington. The more traditional dining room features the warmth of a crackling fire and hand-hewn beams. The glassed-in porch provides candlelite elegance for your evening meal or hearty doses of sunshine to get you off to a cheery start in the morning. The inn boasts recommendations from leading travel and food magazines for its fine dining and selection of California and French wines. Cinnamon spiced shrimp, duck pate, and stuffed mushrooms are a few of the appetizer selections which are followed by inventive and traditional entree choices including raspberry duckling, veal and sun-dried tomatoes, rack of lamb, and Black Angus sirloin steak. The menu also includes chicken, pasta, seafood, and fish. Fresh-baked bread and an array of gourmet desserts round out the dining experience. A full and hearty country breakfast is served each morning. Becky does all the baking for the inn and at breakfast time that includes freshly baked muffins and pastry. Eggs, waffles, pancakes, French toast, and a selection of juices and fresh fruit are standard breakfast choices.

The inn's seventeen guest rooms are furnished with antiques and other fine pieces. Pretty lace curtains, rocking chairs, fresh flowers, and oriental rugs are found in many of the guest rooms. All of the rooms are very bright and many have views. The inn offers a family suite with a private entrance. It has a fully equipped kitchen, a large living room with cable television, and a deck overlooking the White Mountains. It comfortably sleeps up to four adults plus children. It's located in the back of the inn with easy access to the pool, swingset, sandbox, and cross-country ski trails. Other rooms that work well for families have two double beds and a private bath with tub. A king bedded room has enough space to accommodate two roll-aways. Each guest room has its own sink which is extremely helpful when sharing a bath and for those busy mornings when everyone is getting ready at once.

Your family will not be at a loss for things to do in the area. In fact, you will probably have a hard time deciding which activities you'll have to eliminate. The White Mountains National Forest is an outdoor enthusiasts playground with abundant opportunities for hiking, fishing, swimming, and bicycling during the warmer months while winter activities include alpine and cross-country skiing, sledding, ice skating, snowshoeing, and snowmobiling. Year round there's outlet shopping, antiquing, and scenic road tours. The region is also packed with family-fun amusements. Story Land and Heritage-New Hampshire in nearby Glen are two of the area's primary attractions. The Mount Washington Cog Railway, Six Gun City, and Santa's Village are other fun-spots.

Whether your family vacation in the White Mountains Region is fast paced or laid back, The 1785 Inn will provide the comforts of home in a relaxing scenic setting.

Accommodations: 17 guest rooms, 12 with private baths. Roll-aways, high chairs, and booster seats available.

Rates: $69-$159, double occupancy, B&B. Extra persons, $20; children, $10. Family Suite, $99-$179 EP. Weekly rate for suite is $550, except for Christmas week is $750.

Methods of Payment: Cash, personal check, traveler's check, and major credit cards.

Dates of Operation: Open all year.

Children: Appropriate for all ages.

Activities/Facilities: Hiking, fishing, canoeing, swimming, shopping, tennis, golf, skiing, sledding, and ice skating. Nearby family attractions and amusements. The inn's six acres of lawns and gardens also includes an in-ground swimming pool, swingset, sand box, and volleyball.

Philbrook Farm Inn

Innkeepers: The Leger and Philbrook Families
Telephone: (603) 466-3831 or 466-3428
Address: 881 North Road
*   Shelburne, NH 03581*

Leave the harried city life behind and escape to the Philbrook Farm Inn. Located on 1000 acres in the northern White Mountains, miles from any intrusions, this huge old inn offers an idyllic welcome to travelers who make the effort to get there.

Five generations of Philbrooks have provided generous and hospitable service to visitors since 1861. The main building is an imposing three story wooden structure with a multitude of shutters, dormers, and porches. The east and west sections have been added over the years but the center section dates to 1834. Set on the edge of a gently sloping hillside, guests enjoy a pastoral view across fields and the Androscoggin River Valley to the Carter-Moriah and Presidential Mountain ranges beyond. The nineteen guest rooms in the main inn provide an eclectic selection ranging from small and cozy to large and comfortable. Four suite arrangements can be made by combining rooms and baths. Several common rooms on the ground floor provide warm and comfortable gathering places. They are furnished with lots of couches, chairs, and tables and feature fireplaces, lots of books, and an extensive collection of rugs and pillows handmade by generations of Philbrook family members. A downstairs playroom offers ping-pong and pool tables for guests' pleasure. Jigsaw puzzles are usually in progress and a special attraction is a large collection of wooden puzzles hand-crafted by Augustus Philbrook around the turn of the century. The collection of about 100 catalogued, numbered puzzles is a family heirloom available upon request, and probably appropriate for adults or older children who will treat them with care.

In addition to the rooms in the main inn, six summer cottages are sprinkled around the grounds nearby. Like the inn, the cottages offer a wide variety of accommodations. One is named "The Lodge" and has five bedrooms, kitchen, dining room, fireplace, and a living room. What a great option this is for a large family or even two families vacationing together. The other cottages range down in size from The Lodge to a one room plus bath unit with a small porch. Some of the cottages are available with housekeeping arrangements.

Family activities at Philbrook Farm are practically endless. Badminton, horseshoes, croquet, and an outdoor swimming pool are all available in the summer months. Hiking trails meander around the property and connect to the Appalachian Mountain Club trail system and the Appalachian Trail. Wintertime activities include cross-country skiing and snowshoeing right from the front door and downhill skiing available within a short drive. We thought a jigsaw puzzle in front of a warm fireplace would be great for a cold winter day.

Plan to spend a few days at Philbrook Farm and your family will be rejuvenated, refreshed, and anxious to return.

Accommodations: 19 rooms in main inn, some with private baths. 6 summer cottages also available. Cribs, high chairs, and booster seats available.

Rates: Main inn rooms range from $109 to $139 per day, double occupancy, MAP. Cottages range from $124 per day, MAP, to $525 per week on a housekeeping basis (no meals included).

Methods of Payment: Cash, traveler's check, personal check.

Dates of Operation: May 1 through October 31 and December 26 through March 31.

Children: Appropriate for all ages.

Activities/Facilities: Horseback riding, swimming pool, hiking on trails that connect to the Appalachian Trail, nature walks, snowshoeing, cross-country skiing, horseshoes, badminton, and a playroom with ping-pong and pool tables available at the inn. Downhill skiing and mountain climbing in the Presidential Range a short drive from the inn.

Dexter's Inn & Tennis Club

Innkeepers:Michael and Holly Durfor
Telephone: (603) 763-5571, (800) 232-5571
Address: Stagecoach Road
*   Sunapee, NH 03782*

Dexter's Inn and Tennis Club offers guests a slightly refined respite in a beautiful and quiet country setting. The inn's twenty acres of wide lawns, beautiful gardens, and shady sitting areas overlooks dramatic vistas of Lake Sunapee and the surrounding hills including Mount Sunapee to the south. Dexter's dates to 1801 and has been operated as an inn since 1948. Michael and Holly Durfor and their family have run the inn since 1969. Their two young children are frequently about and enjoy mingling with guests and helping out. The Durfors are very friendly and unpretentious hosts and their casual, pleasant style put us right at ease.

The inn is located out in the country and is a bit removed from busy tourist activities and city conveniences, but a wide variety of family attractions are within a short drive. Three golf courses are located nearby and there's no dearth of antique and gift shopping opportunities in the vicinity. Lake Sunapee is a popular summer attraction offering boating, hiking, fishing, and swimming at public beaches within five miles of the inn. Once you settle in at Dexter's, however, you may not feel the need to stray from the property at all. Three outdoor tennis courts are available for guests and the nice big pool is a great place to relax on a sunny afternoon. The Durfors have a tennis pro on staff for those who want to polish their skills or learn the basics. The huge front lawn is perfect for children to run around and play ball or even launch a kite. Croquet sets are available and a shuffleboard court and horseshoe pits are located out back. Hiking and biking in the countryside surrounding the inn are also popular diversions. Hammocks and lawn chairs are nestled around the property for casual conversations or a refreshing afternoon nap.

A converted barn building houses a recreation room with a ping-pong table, bumper pool, and lots of puzzles and games. Dexter's common rooms are numerous and varied. The screened porch overlooking the grounds is a nice place for breakfast. Guests mingle in and out of several other common rooms on the main floor including a library, a living room, and a lounge where drinks are served every evening. A lovely outdoor patio is bedecked with umbrella tables and chairs and is perfect for refreshments after a set of tennis. All the common areas are nicely decorated with chintz-covered couches, imposing natural woodwork, and flowing window treatments. The environment at Dexter's is pleasant and comfortable with just the right touch of casual elegance.

The inn offers seventeen guest rooms plus a two bedroom cottage with a full kitchen and a fireplace. Two of the guest rooms are located upstairs in the barn. These are more rustic and are great for families. All the inn's rooms feature private baths and are decorated with bold country wallpapers, some canopy beds, and semi-formal occasional pieces and accessories.

Dining at Dexter's is a pleasurable experience. A multi-course dinner is served every night except Tuesday in the quaint thirty-seat dining room. Guests can choose from an early or later sitting time and a separate room can be used for families if desired. Holly sets the menu and offers numerous entrees each evening. Babysitting services can be arranged for parents who enjoy a quiet and gracious evening meal. Full country breakfasts including juices, fresh fruit, and entrees such as eggs benedict or French toast will get your day started right. Michael and Holly are always willing to whip up something special for the kids.

Your family will enjoy a stay at Dexter's. The Durfors offer a refined country atmosphere with a welcome sensitivity to family needs.

Accommodations: 17 guest rooms with private baths and a 2-bedroom cottage. Cribs, high chairs, and booster seats available.

Rates: $130-170, double occupancy, MAP. $35 for children under 12 years in room with parents. $45 for 12 years and older. $5 per day crib charge. Slightly lower B&B rates available May, June, September, and October. Discounts available for longer stays.

Methods of Payment: Cash, traveler's check, personal check preferred. Visa and MasterCard accepted.

Dates of Operation: May through October.

Children: Appropriate for all ages.

Activities/Facilities: Tennis, swimming, lawn games, horse shoes, croquet, shuffleboard available on premises. Hiking, biking, golf, water sports, shopping in immediate vicinity.

The Inn at East Hill Farm

Innkeepers: Dave and Sally Adams
Telephone: (603) 242-6495, (800) 242-6495
Address: Troy, NH 03465

A unique family vacation combining farm life and all the amenities of a small resort awaits you at The Inn at East Hill Farm. Nestled at the base of picturesque Mount Monadnock, the inn offers year round activities in what's known as New Hampshire's "Currier and Ives" corner.

Innkeepers Dave and Sally Adams along with the help of their adult children and friendly staff provide their guests with abundant opportunities for endless fun. The inn's summer family vacation season is their busiest and offers warm weather activities for all ages. Two outdoor swimming pools and a wading pool for toddlers, rowboats and paddle boats for use at the pond, fishing, tennis, volleyball, and a small swingset are all to be enjoyed on the grounds at East Hill. Once a week guests go on a field-trip to the inn's private beach on Silver Lake nearby. It has several boats, canoes, float with diving board, docks, sun deck, and a cabin for changing. Speed boat rides and waterskiing are also available and a cookout lunch is provided. For those guests with an appetite for the rugged outdoors, the inn leads a guided tour to the summit of Mount Monadnock. The trek takes about four hours to complete and the inn provides a brown bag lunch.

Guests are welcome to lend a hand in early morning or afternoon chores on the farm. Feeding the animals, gathering eggs, and milking the cow are popular with the younger set. Horseback riding and hay rides are also available.

Daily activities including arts and crafts and story hour are planned for children during the busy summer season and on weekends in the winter. A game room with video machines and a pool table and a lounge with television and arcade games are favorites for the young and old alike.

Winter is a special time at East Hill Farm. Starting in mid-January, the baby lambs are born. Cross-country ski trails are well groomed and ice skating, sledding, and sleigh rides are all part of the winter frolic. An indoor heated pool and whirlpool help to relieve sore muscles from a day's activities. A friendly bit of conversaton can always be found with other guests around the cozy fire. Skiing at nearby Temple mountain is known for its family-friendly slopes.

The Inn at East Hill Farm is famous for its homemade country cooking. Three meals a day are served in the large dining room.

The familiar ringing of the dinner bell brings guests scurrying from the inn's one hundred and fifty acres. In the tradition of the American Plan, families are seated at the same table with the same waitperson. In the summer, poolside barbeques are a big hit.

The inn offers a wide variety of accommodations. They range from the beautiful new Sugar House with five guest rooms and a shared living room to motel-like rooms in the Trail's End. Grandmother's Attic offers old-fashioned charm while the 1950's-style cottages are comfortable and simply furnished.

Catering to families by offering delicious hearty meals, clean and comfortable accommodations, and endless hours of year round indoor and outdoor fun has been the focus at The Inn at East Hill Farm for over two decades. This is a place where all families will feel more than welcome in a setting surely to create lasting memories.

Accommodations: 60 guest rooms, all with private baths.

Rates: $62-$85, per person, double occupancy, AP. Children 5 to 18 years of age, $44-$60. Children ages 2, 3, and 4, $22-$30. Children under 2 stay free. Rates based on a stay of 5 nights or more. Daily rates available upon request.

Methods of Payment: Cash, personal check, traveler's check, Discover, MasterCard, and Visa.

Dates of Operation: Open all year.

Children: Appropriate for all ages.

Activities/Facilities: Swimming, fishing, boating, waterskiing, hiking, tennis, billiards, farm animals, cross-country skiing and more.
Indoor/outdoor pools, whirlpool, sauna, game room, gift shop, and ice skating rink.

Rhode Island

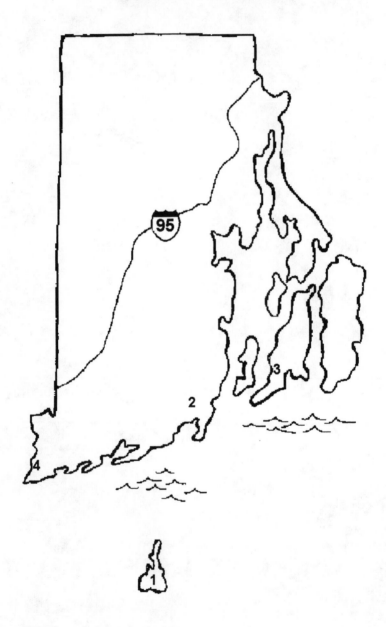

Contents

The 1661 Inn

Innkeepers: Joan and Justin Abrams, Rita and Steve Draper
Telephone: (401) 466-2421, (401) 466-2063
Address: One Spring Street
            Block Island, RI 02807

Block Island offers its visitors serenity, beauty and a host of experiences and adventures for families to partake in, with its own brand of hospitality and "secluded tranquility." In 1969, the Abrams family discovered this treasure of an inn while on one of their many sailing trips to Block Island. Joan and Justin Abrams, along with their three children Rita, Mark, and Rick, took great care in restoring the inn, consulting many books for authentic New England decor. The inn was renamed The 1661 Inn in honor of the year Block Island was settled by New England colonists. The Abrams' have named their guest rooms after some of the early settlers. The 1661 Inn is a lovely inn reminiscent of a bygone era with antiques and Early American paintings.

Many modern day comforts can be found in the guest rooms. The main building houses nine spacious and very comfortable rooms. Many have jacuzzis and eight have their own private decks and ocean views. The 1661 Inn Guest House offers an additional nine cozy rooms just a short walk through a flower garden from the inn. The newest addition to the inn is the Nicholas Ball Cottage. It is a replica of St. Anne's by the Sea Episcopal Church, a building destroyed in the hurricane of 1938. Three sizable suites with fireplaces, jacuzzis, queen size sleeper sofas, microwave ovens, and refrigerators are available here. Two of the suites also have lofts which could double as a play area for children or a private respite for their parents. The Abrams' daughter Rita and her husband Steve Draper, who are actively involved with the planning and day to day innkeeping duties, also have three children and know the importance of making youngsters feel comfortable.

The lawns are expansive, with plenty of room for running around, kite flying, or relaxing while enjoying the breathtaking view of the Atlantic. Your kids won't have trouble spotting the swingset and sandbox at the bottom of the sloping lawn. Across the road, you'll find the inn's petting animal farm. With a little chatter and a few muffins, the goats will come running. There are llamas, cows, donkeys, and ducks, too.

Each morning of your stay you'll be treated to an extravagant breakfast buffet. Eggs, homemade corned beef hash, baked blue fish, muffins, pancakes, and breakfast meats are a sample of this bountiful feast. Guests can enjoy their breakfast inside the dining room or outside under the canopy covered deck. The inn also has a complimentary wine and nibble hour.

Block Island was recently designated as one of the ten last unspoiled places on the earth. There are fresh and saltwater ponds to explore and wide, long beaches where you can build sand castles and hunt for shells. The Mohegan Bluffs are a natural wonder you won't want to miss. These intriguing clay bluffs, towering 200 feet above the Atlantic, can be found at the southern tip of the island. Put on your climbing shoes and hike to the top. You won't be sorry. Bicycling and walking are the preferred modes of transportation on the island. Bicycles can be rented at many shops. There are many places to dine. Whether you want a picnic lunch for the beach, or want to don your finest apparel, you'll find it all here. We recommend Ballard's - just down the road from The 1661. Its large dining room, deck, and private beach make for a fun dining experience. They also have a children's menu.

The 1661 Inn is a special place located on a very special island. Experiencing the two together will leave lasting memories.

Accommodations: 21 rooms. Private baths in The 1661 Inn, and Nicholas Ball Cottage. Four of the nine guest rooms in The Guest House have shared bath, five with private baths.

Rates: $65-$325, double occupancy, B&B. Children 5 years and younger, no charge. Third person in room, $25.

Methods of Payment: Cash, traveler's check, personal check, major credit cards.

Dates of Operation: The 1661 Inn open April 1 thru Nov. 12. The 1661 Guest House and the Nicholas Ball Cottage open year-round.

Children: Appropriate for all ages.

Activities/Facilities: Swingset, sandbox, petting farm, kitchenettes, jacuzzis, and private decks. Nearby beaches, bicycling, shelling, and restaurants.

The Blue Dory Inn

Innkeepers: Ann and Ed Loedy
Telephone: (401) 466-5891, (800) 992-7290
Address: P.O. Box 488
Dodge Street
Block Island, RI 02807

Quaint accommodations right on the beach in a small island village are graciously offered at The Blue Dory Inn. Innkeepers Ann and Ed Loedy have created a beautiful retreat that is at once charmingly Victorian and wonderfully comfortable. The inn's location in the village's central historic district offers more than convenient access to shops, restaurants, and services (it's within a block of the ferry landing). And it backs directly onto Crescent Beach, one of Block Island's many wide, clean beaches.

Guest rooms are comprised of eleven rooms in the main building plus three cottages just outside the back door. All the buildings are connected by a cozy patio area that serves as a primary mingling place for guests in summer. The Burnell Dodge Suite, located in the main building, and The Cottage building offer the best accommodations for families. The Dodge Suite has a double bed room and an adjoining sitting room with a day bed that can be configured as two twin beds or a king bed. This suite, like the entire inn, is beautifully decorated in Victorian style. Plump, flowery quilts and windows ensconced in flowing drapes and sheers give the antique furnishings and fixtures a most appropriate air of elegance. The Cottage is a two room efficiency that is virtually on the beach and can sleep up to six or seven in comfort and privacy. Cribs and roll-aways are available and would fit easily into a number of the other rooms.

Common rooms are located in the main building. A beautiful parlor at the front of the house has lots of large windows and beautiful stained wood trim. It is pleasantly stuffed with antique sofas and chairs and also contains a television. The kitchen and breakfast area is open and considerably more homey. Checkered linens and a profusion of flowers bring cheer to even the most sleepy-eyed morning arrivals. Daily continental breakfasts include fresh breads and pastries, fresh fruits, a variety of juices and herbal teas, and plenty of coffee. Guests can help themselves to the bowl of fresh fruit in the front hallway throughout the day and in the evening Ann or one of her friendly staff members bakes up a fresh batch of cookies.

The Loedys provide towels and beach chairs for their guests and an outdoor refrigerator which is very handy for a day at the beach with a toddler. Ann will outline daytrips with guests and even offers box lunches for those planning a day touring the island's natural attractions. A car is also available for guests to use to circumnavigate the entire island or just run an errand.

The Loedys can also help you arrange guided island tours and bicycle rentals and can suggest numerous ways to make your Block Island vacation a special one. Ann and Ed are happy, outgoing hosts who have created a warm and welcoming hostel for their many satisfied visitors.

Accommodations: 11 guest rooms plus three all-season cottages, all with private baths. Roll-aways and cribs available.

Rates: Guest rooms are $85-$175, double occupancy, B&B. The Dodge Suite and cottages are $110-$265, for up to four guests, B&B. Additional persons, $20. Rates vary by season and lower rates are available October through mid-May.

Methods of Payment: Cash, personal check, traveler's check, MasterCard, Visa, American Express.

Dates of Operation: Open all year.

Children: Appropriate for all ages.

Activities/Facilities: Sandy beach access directly from the inn. Island shops and restaurants are abundant in the immediate vicinity. Mohegan Bluffs, lighthouses, birdwatching, hiking, and bicycling trails, boat rentals and charters, fishing and picnicking are readily accessible. Numerous historic buildings and sites. Holiday events at the inn include "Thanksgiving with Grandma," Halloween hayrides, and moonlight horserides at Christmastime.

Ilverthorpe Cottage

Innkeepers: Chris and John Webb, Jill Raggio
Telephone: (401) 789-2392
Address: 41 Robinson Street,
*   Narragansett, RI 02882*

Ilverthorpe Cottage is a charming B&B with a romantic history reflected in its present day ambiance. In 1896, Edgar O. Watts had the cottage built as a wedding gift for his bride, Jessie. According to their daughter Virginia, Jessie was reading an English novel titled "Ilverthorpe" while the cottage was being built. The home remained in the Watts family until 1983 when it was sold to its present owners. Innkeepers Chris Webb and her husband John, along with her daughter Jill, are gracious hosts and have been offering warm hospitality since then. The setting for this Victorian home is in the heart of Narragansett's historic district just a few blocks from beaches, shops, restaurants, and a movie theatre.

A spacious yard is sprinkled with lovely bedding plants bordering walks and a wraparound porch amidst towering trees. Hallmarks of traditional New England B&B finery adorn each room inside.

Antique furnishings, fresh cut flowers, stenciling, and lace accents abound. Small collectibles of fine porcelain and glass as well as Chris' dried flower arrangements are displayed throughout the B&B. Surprisingly, our two small children enjoyed these small treasures with their eyes.

Four cozy and inviting guest rooms are located on the second floor of the cottage. The rooms are tastefully decorated and spotless. Our room had a king bed and private bath. There were pretty old-fashioned children's gowns hung on the walls and beautiful bird's eye maple furnishings. There was room for a roll-away and our portable crib, too. If your children are older you may want to put them in the room with twin beds. This room along with a double bedded room share a large bath. Another four poster canopied double bedroom also has a private bath.

In the morning, we were awakened by the aroma of fresh bread baking (Chris omitted the raisins at our daughter's request). Fresh fruit, juice, and apple pancakes rounded out the fare. Many more enticing breakfast specialties like breakfast pizza, blintzes, and French egg puff are prepared to pamper each guest. Guests may enjoy this bountiful feast in the casual elegance of the family dining room or on the screened portion of the wraparound porch. It's the newest addition to the B&B and makes for a cheery spot to start your day.

Narragansett is centrally located between the Westerly and Watch Hill area and Newport. Activities abound along this lovely stretch of shoreline. A day trip to Block Island complete with ferry ride may also be on your agenda. Fishing in the nearby village of Galilee, a day at one of Narragansett's beaches, bicycling, or investigating the history of this historic town's enormous turn-of-the-century stone towers will round out your family's day.

At the end of your busy day, come home to Ilverthorpe and take refuge in one of the wicker rockers on the veranda while enjoying a glass of complimentary wine.

Accommodations: 4 guest rooms, 2 with private bath, 2 with shared bath.

Rates: $60-$80, double occupancy, B&B. Roll-away available.

Dates of Operation: May through October.

Methods of Payment: Cash, traveler's check, personal check.

Children: Appropriate for all ages.

Activities/Facilities: Nearby beaches, shops, restaurants, and movie theatre. Also bicycling, summer theatre, tennis, golf, sailing, fishing, and antiquing. Foxwoods Casino.

Yankee Peddler Inn

Innkeeper: Debra Smith
Telephone: (401) 846-1323
Address: 113 Touro St.
Newport, RI 02840

If, like many families, you are of the impression that Newport is for couples and singles only, but are longing to spend a couple of days touring the historic mansions and shopping at quaint little boutiques and gift shops along the wharf, don't despair. We found many local attractions for families and a wonderful haven to call home during your stay, the Yankee Peddler Inn. The inn is located just three short blocks from Newport's bustling harbor. The inn itself is a lovely nineteenth century Greek Revival. A charming cottage just across the courtyard is also part of the inn.

In residence innkeeper Debra Smith and her youthful staff are very attentive to their guests' needs and requests. Parents traveling with children will appreciate their energy and their willingness to help.

The inn boasts nineteen guest rooms. Each features period furnishings, original art works, and Laura Ashley and Ralph Lauren bedding. Fourteen rooms in the main inn are all very large and, with the exception of two rooms, have private baths. Larger families or parents seeking a little more privacy will love the two bedroom suites. Other rooms have queen beds and one twin, two double beds, or one queen size bed for parents traveling with an infant who just need room for a portable crib. The cottage houses an additional five cozy guest rooms which are less spacious than those in the main inn, but have rather large bathrooms.

In the morning you will be treated to a continental breakfast of bagels, muffins, fresh fruit, juices, and coffee served in the breakfast room. Cable television, newspapers, and brochures of Newport's events and activities are also located in this common area. The inn also has a large, furnished sun deck with a picturesque view of Newport's harbor. The deck is a favorite gathering spot where the Inn's guests share in a bit of conversation and imbibe in a beverage. The inn also provides off street parking for their guests' convenience.

Newport has many events and activities scheduled throughout the year. In summer, you can choose from yachting and boat shows, or touring mansions and Colonial homes. The cliff walk with its rocky terrain provides for an adventurous outing in any season. Christmas in Newport is a month long affair and includes a wonderful craft fair. Newport is also home of the Tennis Hall of Fame. Great restaurants, art shows, music festivals, and antiquing are all to be found in this charming town.

You'll treasure your memories of times spent in Newport and at the Yankee Peddler Inn.

Accommodations: 19 rooms, all but 2 with private bath. Roll-aways available.

Rates: $45-$115, double occupancy, B&B. Children, $5. $10 for additional adult in same room.

Methods of Payment: Cash, traveler's check, personal check, and major credit cards.

Dates of Operation: Open all year.

Children: Appropriate for all ages.

Activities/Facilities: Mansion tours, historic churches, Tennis Hall of Fame, art shows and galleries, professional and amateur theater, cliff walk, yachting events, boat shows, harbor cruises, restaurants, and much more. Off street parking.

Grandview Bed and Breakfast

Innkeeper: *Pat Grande*
Telephone: *(401) 596-6384, (800) 447-6384*
Address: *212 Shore Road,*
Westerly, RI 02891-3923

Comfort and hospitality are what innkeeper Pat Grande offers her guests at Grandview B&B. Upon arriving at Grandview, we met a couple of loyal guests who had nothing but accolades of praise for Pat and her B&B. This stately, turn-of-the-century home offers a marvelous ocean view and a magnificent wrap-around stone porch for guests to enjoy. Parents of young children will also appreciate the understated decor and comfort of this B&B. The living room is bright and gives one the feeling of being at home. Relax on the oversized couch with plush, down-filled cushions in front of the beautiful stone fireplace, or catch up on some news or reading in the family room which also houses a player piano and table games.

Ten cozy guest rooms decorated with a potpourri of furnishings offer families a number of options. Rooms with double beds can accommodate a roll-away or crib as can rooms with twin beds. Double and twin bedded rooms can be combined to create a family suite like the one we stayed in. Our rooms were actually across the hall from one another but were connected by an enclosed sun porch with comfy furnishings, a small television, and a portable refrigerator. Our kids loved this little room and parents will enjoy the privacy it provides between the rooms. Worth noting was the child sized roll-away which our daughter slept in. She loved the children's bedding on it also.

Wake up to freshly baked muffins or bread, fresh fruit, juice, coffee, and cereal. This continental breakfast, served buffet style, can be enjoyed in the cheery enclosed sunporch or on the wrap-around stone porch. You'll have a chance to visit with other guests and with Pat, who is an engaging conversationalist.

Over your last cup of coffee you may want to plan your day. There are many activities you'll want to consider. A day at the beach is a must. There are a number of private and public ones to chose from. Watch Hill is just minutes away and while there, your children will delight in one of the country's oldest merry-go-rounds. Golf, tennis, and good restaurants are also nearby. A day trip might include the Mystic Marinelife Aquarium or a ferry boat ride to Block Island. Westerly and its neighboring towns have too many excursions and sights to see in one visit. You'll want to return to this splendid area and to Grandview B&B over and over again. I know we will.

Accommodations: 10 rooms, 6 with private bath, 4 with shared bath. Roll-aways and inflatable mattresses available.

Rates: $65-$95, double occupancy, B&B. $15 charge for each additional person.

Methods of Payment: Cash, traveler's check, personal check, and major credit cards.

Dates of Operation: Open all year.

Children: Appropriate for all ages.

Activities/Facilities: Nearby beaches, tennis, and golf. Short drive to Mystic, and Foxwoods Casino, CT, Newport, and Watch Hill, RI.

Shelter Harbor Inn

Innkeepers: Jim Dey
Telephone: (401) 322-8883
Address: 10 Wagner Road
             Westerly, RI 02891

A sun-filled day at a private beach, an afternoon game of croquet, followed by an elegant dining experience and a late night
dip in the hot tub characterize a stay at the Shelter Harbor Inn.
This lovely inn is located near Block Island Sound and
Quonochontaug Pond. The inn's own private beach stretches
two miles across beautiful shoreline. Originally a farmhouse
built in the early 1800's, the inn has been lovingly restored and
expresses a casual elegance throughout. Innkeeper Jim Dey
offers friendly hospitality in a relaxing atmosphere.

Guests have a choice of twenty-three comfortable and spotless
rooms. Nine guest rooms can be found in the main house. Many
of these rooms have fireplaces and private decks. The barn also
has ten guest rooms. The large central living room on the upper

level makes the barn an ideal location for family reunions and informal business retreats. The charming carriage house has four additional guest rooms all with fireplaces. Several rooms have sleeper sofas and room for a roll-away or crib. All guest rooms have private baths.

The inn features elegant country dining and invites guests and local friends to enjoy "traditional New England fare." A children's menu includes many favorites for the less sophisticated palate. You may choose to dine in one of three separate rooms. The original dining room is warm and cozy with its large hearth and exposed beam ceiling. The sunporch is bright and in the evening is quite elegant. More recently, a larger dining room with lots of windows has been added. This is a perfect spot to view the inn's well maintained gardens. In the morning, enjoy a hearty breakfast before venturing out. The inn also prepares box lunches for those making a day of it at the beach.

Shelter Harbor offers a number of facilities including a beautifully manicured croquet court, a private beach, paddle tennis courts, a large hot tub, and several cozy spots to relax, read, or visit with other guests. Nearby activities include golf, tennis, boating, and bicycling. Day trips to Mystic, CT, Block Island, and Newport, RI will also prove to be fun and interesting for the whole family. Many more attractions can be found in this coastal area rich in beauty and simplicity. Whatever your plans may include, Shelter Harbor Inn will embrace your weary family with comfortable accommodations and warm hospitality.

Accommodations: 23 rooms, all with private bath. Crib and roll-aways available.

Rates: $76-$116, double occupancy, B&B. Children under 12 years, $15. Extra adult in same room, $25.

Methods of Payment: Cash, traveler's check, personal check, and major credit cards.

Dates of Operation: Open all year.

Children: Appropriate for all ages.

Activities/Facilities: 2 mile stretch of private beach, croquet court, two paddle tennis courts, large hot tub and locker room. Breakfast, lunch, and dinner are served daily to inn guests and to the public. Nearby golf, tennis, boating, bicycling, and many local area attractions and day trips.

Woody Hill Bed & Breakfast

Innkeeper: *Dr. Ellen Madison*
Telephone: *(401) 322-0452*
Address: *149 South Woody Hill Road*
              Westerly, RI 02891

Ellen Madison describes her bed and breakfast as "close to the beaten path and yet not on it". Westerly, Rhode Island is a popular summer vacation destination tucked into the southwest corner of the state. It is a rather hectic and commercialized area offering a wide variety of dining and entertainment opportunities in addition to some splendid beaches. You can enjoy all of the local amenities and then retreat to a quiet, spacious place to relax, unwind, and recharge at Woody Hill. Ellen's home is a modern gambrel cape set on a twenty acre hillside of wide lawns, open pastures, and informal gardens. This former farming property has been in her family for generations. It is located just two miles from the ocean.

Although the house is modern, it contains many features of a colonial antique. Open hearth fireplaces, twelve over twelve windows, exposed beams, and wide pine floors together with old-fashioned trim work and appointments give Woody Hill the feel of an original settler's homestead. Two of the four guest rooms would be great for families. Room Three includes a canopy double bed, a three-quarter bed and a sofa. It is a spacious room with a private entrance and direct access to the 40-foot swimming pool out back. For larger families, it can be combined with the adjoining Library Room which has a queen hide-a-bed, walls of books, and shuttered windows. This combination could easily sleep six. Room One contains two double beds, one of which is a beautiful four-poster tucked in an alcove for partial privacy.

In addition to roaming the fields and lawns, your children will surely enjoy the swimming pool. The pool area also has a screened porch with tables and chairs and a refrigerator plus two changing rooms. Breakfast is hearty. Ellen serves the morning meal in the Keeping Room which is reminiscent of colonial kitchens with an open hearth fireplace with bake oven and a large wooden table. The fare usually features French toast, waffles with strawberries, or other entree plus a variety of accompaniments including fresh fruit with ginger sauce, hot apple crisp with whipped cream, juices, and coffee. Ellen has been an English teacher for almost thirty years and she has some interesting accessories around the house that our children enjoyed discovering. There's a collection of antique eye glasses and an antique correcting chair used in classrooms of old. We really enjoyed Ellen's warm hospitality. Her unique accommodations make a visit to the coast a relaxing, enriching family experience.

Accommodations: 4 guest rooms, 3 with private baths. Cots, cribs, and high chair available.

Rates: $60-$105, double occupancy, B&B. Extra persons, $10. Lower rates available during off season.

Methods of Payment: Cash, personal check, traveler's check.

Dates of Operation: Open all year.

Children: Appropriate for all ages.

Activities/Facilities: Swimming pool and acres of lawns, fields, and woods at the inn. Full array of ocean-side attractions very close by. Newport, RI and Mystic, CT are within an hours drive. Ferrys to Block Island depart nearby as well.

Vermont

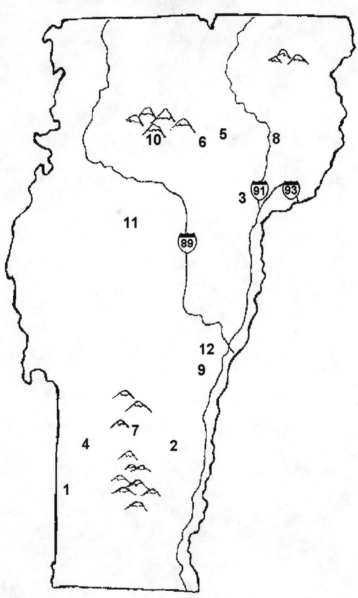

3 91 93

89

Contents

Hill Farm Inn

Innkeepers: Joanne and George Hardy
Telephone: (802) 375-2269, (800) 882-2545, Fax (802) 375-9918
Address: R.R. 2
*   Box 2015*
*   Arlington, VT 05250*

The Hill Farm Inn has been welcoming guests for more than ninety years. The inn is located on a quiet road a short distance from southern Vermont's busy Route 7A and is a comfortable, refreshing hospice for traveling families. Surrounded by 50 acres of farmland with a mile of frontage on the famed Battenkill River, Hill Farm Inn enjoys spectacular mountain views in every direction. Innkeepers Joanne and George Hardy provide a warm, laid back style of hospitality very fitting to this bucolic setting. They also feel a strong responsibility to provide a place where families can vacation and relax together.

Visitors can choose from a variety of accommodations at Hill Farm. The main building dates to the 1820's and houses all the common rooms and guest rooms upstairs. Several of these work well for families with plenty of room for roll-aways or cribs. A suite features a queen bed, a living room with wood stove and convertible couch, a kitchenette, and a porch entrance. The 1790 Guest House contains several more guest rooms. We stayed in the Lilac Suite which has a cozy living room with convertible couch, a kitchenette, television, a full private bath, a bedroom with queen sized bed, and a private porch and entrance. If you prefer even more privacy, there are four seasonal cabins arranged on the spacious lawn next to the inn. One of these, the Butternut, has two bedrooms and is popular with families. Public rooms include a large country dining room and a well appointed living room, both on the first floor of the main building. Low, beamed ceilings, slightly curvy plaster walls, and windows and doors a bit out of square authenticate the historic significance of Hill Farm. The living room has comfortable overstuffed furnishings, a piano, lots of books, games, puzzles, magazines, and a big fireplace. The dining room is furnished with several plain wooden tables spaciously arranged and opens to a wide screened porch overlooking the large front lawn.

The Hardys serve up a wonderful country breakfast. Begin with a choice of four fresh juices and steaming bran muffins. Then, oatmeal with brown sugar, your favorite cold cereal or their celebrated Hill Farm Granola. Eggs cooked any style, buttermilk pancakes or old fashioned french toast with a choice of local bacon or sausage round out the fare. It's just the kind of food you would expect on a farm. Dinners are avaiable, by advance reservation.

There is no shortage of family activities in the area. The Battenkill River flows within a quarter mile of the inn and is a haven for canoeists and fly fishing addicts. Mt. Equinox dominates the valley between Manchester and Arlington and a toll road to its summit provides great views of the surrounding Taconic and Green mountains. Loads of shopping and family entertainment facilities are within a short drive. Swimming, hiking, and biking opportunities abound in nearby parks and recreation areas and plenty of downhill and cross-country skiing is available in wintertime. A number of historic sites are nearby including Hildene, Robert Todd Lincoln's former residence. The Hardys belong to a local historical group which publishes a guide to the region including recommended sites and activities for all seasons and any kind of weather. Each guest room at the inn is furnished with a copy and we recommend that you use it as a planning reference.

Hill Farm Inn is historic, comfortable, and spacious. The Hardy's commitment to this farm and the local community shine through in their warm hospitality and we recommend a visit.

Accommodations: 13 rooms, 8 with private baths, and 4 seasonal cottages with private baths. Roll-aways, cribs, high chairs available.

Rates: $75-$125, double occupancy, B&B. Children 2 to 5 years, $10; 6 to 12 years, $15; over 12 years, $25; porta-crib, $5.

Methods of Payment: Cash, traveler's check, personal check, Visa, MasterCard, American Express, Discover.

Dates of Operation: Open all year.

Children: Appropriate for all ages.

Activities/Facilities: Swingset, lawn games, board games, and puzzles available at inn. A preponderance of hiking, skiing, fishing, boating, biking, river sports, shopping, and sightseeing in the area.

West Mountain Inn

Innkeepers: Wes and Mary Ann Carlson
Telephone: (802) 375-6516
Address: River Road
*   Arlington, VT 05250*

Gracefully nestled on a hillside overlooking the Battenkill River, the West Mountain Inn lures its guests with gracious hospitality, exceptionally hearty meals, and truly imaginative and comfortable accommodations. Over fifteen years ago, innkeepers Wes and Mary Ann Carlson escaped the suburbs of New York and set out to create a country inn where people could come to relax and enjoy nature's tranquil effects. Their success is largely attributable to the genuine and warm hospitality they extend to each guest. The Carlsons employ a wonderful staff committed to personal service. 150 acres of woods and sprawling lawns afford outdoor enthusiasts plenty of opportunities to commune with nature. We spotted a couple of cardinals who had come to eat at the busy bird feeding station. Semi-tame lop-eared rabbits roam the grounds freely as do chipmunks who come to feast on the spilled bird seed. The inn's most popular animal attractions, however, are the llamas. Not exactly indigenous to this region, the llamas create a special curiosity among guests. Wes is the primary shepherd of this captivating herd.

Guest rooms offer comfortable accommodations combined with unique and well designed floor plans. The rooms range from dramatic to romantic and cozy. The Norman Rockwell Treetop Room will delight younger children. Three pullman-type compartments complete with bed, curtains, and even a light make curling up with a story book especially fun. A queen size bed for parents makes this a great room for families. The Rockwell Kent Suite with its cathedral ceiling, fireplace, and large sitting area provides a family plenty of room to relax. A king size bed and loft add to this suite's dramatic effect. The Daniel Webster Suite offers a bit more privacy for families. Two separate rooms with one behind a mirrored door give parents and children alike their own space. The Grandma Moses Suite has a cozy sitting room with a fireplace, queen sofa sleeper, and queen size bed. The Cottage in the Pines is another option for families. It sits below the main inn and houses two guest rooms and a common area. A handicapped accessible room is found on the first floor. The common area has a fully outfitted country kitchen and a cozy living room. Fresh fruit, a chocolate llama, and one of Wes' home grown African violets are found in each of the inn's rooms to be enjoyed and taken home as a remembrance of your stay.

A full country breakfast with fresh baked goodies and hearty entrees will prepare you for exploring southern Vermont's many attractions. After a busy day, guests are treated to a wonderful selection of appetizers, entrees, and desserts for dinner. Babysitters can be arranged for parents seeking a leisurely dining experience. The cookie jar is always full for snacking in between.

The Historic Inns of Norman Rockwell's Vermont is a local association of innkeepers that the Carlsons belong to which has published an informative guidebook to assist guests in planning their activities. "Finding Your Way in Southern Vermont" highlights and summarizes area attractions. You won't want to leave the inn without it.

The Carlson's invite you to enjoy their special "peace of Vermont" and we recommend West Mountain Inn for a memorable family vacation.

Accommodations: 15 guest rooms, all with private baths. Cribs and roll-aways available. 1 barrier free room.

Rates: $139-$184, main inn, double occupancy, MAP. Children 4 years and younger, $10; 5 to 12 years, $30. Additional adult in same room, $54-$64.

Methods of Payment: Cash, traveler's check, personal check, Visa, MasterCard, American Express, and Discover.

Dates of Operation: Open all year.

Children: Appropriate for all ages.

Activities/Facilities: Library with games, books, and puzzles. Game room with cribbage, chess, checkers, and backgammon. Nearby fishing, canoeing, bicycling, hiking, downhill and cross-country skiing. Revolutionary War battlefield tour and Norman Rockwell Gallery. Shopping and restaurants nearby.

The Hugging Bear Inn and Shoppe

Innkeepers: Georgette, Diane, and Paul Thomas
Telephone: (802) 875-2412 (800) 325-0519
Address: Main Street
*   Chester, VT 05143*

All sorts of wonderful, cuddly bears will greet your every turn at The Hugging Bear Inn. Every room in this beautiful old Victorian home is liberally decorated with bears of every imaginable size and shape. Georgette Thomas chose this theme when she first opened the inn in 1982. Many of her guests, children and adults alike, were so taken with the teddy bears which adorned their beds that they offered to buy them as mementos of their stay. From these inauspicious beginnings, a house full of bears and a bustling bear theme gift shop have developed, and Georgette Thomas has cemented her reputation as a warm and giving host.

In recent years, Georgette has been assisted by her son, Paul, and his wife, Diane, who now reside on the property as well. There are six guest rooms with private baths located on the second floor. Each is spacious, comfortable, and homey. The furnishings are sturdy and clean, sort of like the extra bedroom at Grandma's house. Elegance and hauty pretense are overlooked in favor of casual, home style comfort. Georgette's friendly and accommodating personality is reflected throughout the inn. She was more than happy to read our daughter her bedtime story and she relishes her youthful visitors.

The inn's main floor consists of three public rooms. At the base of the grand oak staircase leading to the guest rooms is a large living room with Victorian window coverings and furnishings. A TV with VCR is available for guests to enjoy, but you may have to move a resting teddy bear or one of Georgette's two cats before settling into a comfortable chair. A wide selection of children's movies is on hand. Adjoining the living room is a smaller library/den room. Floor to ceiling built-in shelves ring the room. They are virtually stuffed with books, games, puzzles, toys, and teddy bears. Our children were more than occupied as they made new discoveries and met the other young guests. The dining room features a large hardwood table and plenty of space to move about.

Breakfasts at The Hugging Bear are hearty and delicious. We particularly recommend the apple cinnamon pancakes which are the specialty of the house. Guests can also choose from a variety of egg dishes, blueberry pancakes, or French toast. A full complement of breakfast meats, juices, coffee, and fruit round out the fare. Don't be afraid to ask for seconds as Georgette rues the thought of a guest leaving hungry. She entertained everyone at the table with her impromptu bear puppet show which included antique puppets and a gentle environmental message.

The gift shop is located at the back of the inn and contains enough bear-aphernalia for the most enthusiastic teddy bear fan. Georgette reminded us that teddy bears are the single most collected item in the world and her wares include many Artist Bears and limited edition products. She also stocks a good selection of souvenirs, puzzles, and books.

We enjoyed our stay at The Hugging Bear and your family will find Georgette's sweet, kind manner and her unique establishment to be enchanting and enjoyable, too.

Accommodations: 6 guest rooms with private baths. Rollaways, cribs, high chairs, booster seats available.

Rates: $75-$85, double occupancy, B&B. Extra persons, $20; under 14 years of age, $10.

Methods of Payment: Cash, traveler's check, personal check, MasterCard, Visa, Discover, and American Express.

Dates of Operation: Open all year.

Children: Appropriate for all ages.

Activities/Facilities: Golf, tennis, fishing, swimming, playground, hiking, summer theatre nearby. Nordic and alpine skiing, sledding, winter festivals in the vicinity. Historic districts, scenic drives, shopping.

Broadview Farm
Bed & Breakfast

Innkeepers: Joe and Molly Newell
Telephone: (802) 748-9902
Address: Danville, VT
*   RFD #2, Box 153*
*   St. Johnsbury, VT 05819*

Most of us like to get away from it all when we go on vacation. If you are feeling the itch to get really away, away from everything, away from any semblance of city life, you might consider a visit to Broadview Farm. Located on a winding dirt road north of Danville, Vermont, this is a working farm that has been in the same family since 1900 and has taken guests and summer refugees from cities throughout the northeast since the late 1800's. A family could get consumed by the country style existence for days or weeks and forget that St. Johnsbury and Interstate 91 are less than ten miles away.

Vermont

Joe and Molly Newell carry on the great Vermont tradition of doing a little of this and a little of that to get by. They raise Christmas Trees. They raise animals. They produce over 500 gallons of maple syrup each year (requiring about 20,000 gallons of raw sap!). And they take limited numbers of guests from June through October and January to March. It's the kind of place that you might want to tell only a few special friends about. Too much attention might threaten the peaceful atmosphere.

There are four guest rooms including an apartment with three bedrooms that can easily accommodate five people. The apartment has a private bath and the other rooms share baths. This beautiful dormered gambrel house has wide porches overlooking lawns, pastures, and out buildings and is listed in the National Register of Historic Homes. There is a game room inside with toys, games, and books which is a nice place to settle down after a day of exploring the maple orchard, Christmas tree groves, and barns. The Newells keep a "family" of farm animals including two beautiful Golden Retrievers (who were very gentle with our youngsters), two cats, a couple of cows, and a goat. Your children could occupy themselves with this menagerie all day.

Molly prepares a hearty continental breakfast for guests each morning while Joe tends to the early chores. Blueberry muffins and pancakes, with homemade maple syrup of course, are specialties. There's a lot to do in the area if you feel like venturing from the farm. In the winter, cross-country skiing and snowshoeing is available all around the region (as well as right out the back door) and Burke Mountain Ski Resort is within thirty minutes drive. Summer visitors can enjoy country auctions, farmers markets, and craft fairs. There are also plenty of opportunities for swimming, boating, and fishing. The Northeast Kingdom of Vermont is one of New England's most spectacular presenters of the autumnal explosion of foliage color. At a crystal clear altitude of 2000 feet above sea level, Broadview Farm's 350 acres are particularly beautiful to explore at this time of year.

Accommodations: 4 guest rooms including an apartment with 3 bedrooms and a private bath. Other rooms share baths.

Rates: $38-$45, double occupancy, B&B. Apartment sleeps up to five and is $100, B&B.

Methods of Payment: Cash, personal check, traveler's check, MasterCard, Visa.

Dates of Operation: June to mid-October and January through February.

Children: Appropriate for all ages.

Activities/Facilities: Working farm on 350 country acres. Farm animals, maple sugaring, lots of fields and woods. Hiking, fishing, swimming, boating, skiing, and snowmobiling available in the area. Antique shops, restaurants, craft fairs, and museums located nearby.

Barrows House

Innkeepers: Jim and Linda McGinnis
Telephone: (802) 867-4455 (800) 639-1620
Address: Dorset, VT 05251

At Barrows House, you will find the charm of country romance while your children will delight in the twelve park-like acres of grounds including a large outdoor swimming pool, tennis courts, and badminton courts. Innkeepers Jim and Linda McGinnis warmly welcome families to their inn and provide a host of appropriate sleeping arrangements. The main inn and seven separate white clapboard buildings with shutters and dormers grace well maintained lawns accented with bright flower gardens. Accommodations range from a six bedroom house to a charming single-suite cottage. The Carriage House affords privacy for parents and children alike with a king size bed downstairs and a loft sleeping up to six on the second floor. Many of the rooms have small refrigerators and a couple have kitchen facilities. The rooms are appointed with traditional country furnishings with a touch of elegance. The living room in the main inn is stocked with books, games, and puzzles and has comfortable furnishings, handcrafted lampshades, and original stenciling dating back to the origins of the house. A game room in the basement of Truffles, another guest house, has a pool table and ping-pong table.

Rates at Barrows House include a hearty breakfast and a four course dinner. Fresh fruit, hot and cold cereals, eggs any style served with homefries, homemade buttermilk pancakes, and French toast are typical breakfast items with Vermont smoked bacon, sausage, and Canadian bacon rounding out the fare. Dinners at Barrows House are special. They include hot or cold appetizers, homemade bread and salad, and a wonderful selection of entrees followed by a sinful choice of desserts. Imaginative use of the freshest and finest ingredients provides for a distinctive dining experience. The inn's cozy and fully licensed tavern is a great spot to begin or end your dinner. A children's menu is also available.

Barrows House is located in the quaint little Vermont town of Dorset. Nestled at the foot of the Green Mountain National Forest, Dorset and its neighboring communities afford visitors to this picturesque region a multitude of activities. Hiking, canoeing, fishing, bicycling, and downhill and cross-country skiing are readily available. Summer theatre and outdoor concerts will occupy your late afternoons and evenings. If you're a shop-till-you-drop die-hard then make your way to Manchester where you'll find hours of upscale factory stores. Special attractions for families include the Enchanted Doll House, a toy and miniature shop in Manchester, the Alpine slide at Bromley, and the Billings Farm Museum in nearby Woodstock. Many guests at Barrows House prefer to stay put and enjoy all the inn's amenities, be it sunning at the pool, playing a game of tennis, badminton or croquet, or just curling up with a good book.

Jim and Linda have perfected the art of gracious hospitality at Barrows House. An opportunity to stay at their inn would be a memorable experience for your family.

Accommodations: 28 guest rooms with private baths. Cribs, roll-aways, high chairs, and boosters available.

Rates: $180-$240, double occupancy, MAP. Children's rates available upon request.

Methods of Payment: Cash, traveler's check, or personal check preferred. MasterCard, Discover, American Express, and Visa.

Dates of Operation: Open all year.

Children: Appropriate for all ages .

Activities/Facilities: Outdoor swimming pool, sauna, tennis courts, badminton court, croquet, game room, and bicycles for guests to use. Barrows House can also facilitate family reunions and small group meetings for corporations and organizations. Activities to be found nearby include fishing, canoeing, hiking, bicycling, downhill and cross-country skiing, shopping, and sightseeing.

The Little Lodge at Dorset

Innkeepers: Allan and Nancy Norris
Telephone: (802) 867-4040
Address: P.O. Box 673, Route 30
*   Dorset, VT 05251*

The Little Lodge at Dorset bed and breakfast is a treasure, incon-spicuously tucked away up on a hillside in an idyllic New England village setting. This beautiful white clapboard cottage-like farmhouse dates back to 1810 and is listed in the National Registry of Historic Places. Just beyond the front entrance and down the gently sloping lawn is the B&B's own small trout pond perfect for swimming in the warmer months or ice skating in the winter. Innkeepers Allan and Nancy Norris are grandpar-ents who offer a warm and friendly welcome to families.

The B&B offers several comfortable common rooms. The barn-board den with its inviting window seat and cheery fireplace exudes a warm and homey atmosphere. A good selection of books, a television, board games, a guest refrigerator, and bar setup are also found here. A hexagonal porch and a living room with woodstove and lovely stencil designed wallpaper are additional gathering spots for guests.

The B&B's five guest rooms are furnished with antiques, braided rugs, crocheted or quilted bedcovers, and lace or coordinating curtains. Stenciling and wide floorboards complete the country decor. Two adjoining rooms, the Rose Room and the Berry Vine Room, are ideal for families where parents can enjoy privacy and security knowing their children are safe next door. Cots and a crib can also be arranged for children sleeping in the same room as their parents. The B&B's slanting ceilings and little windows add to each rooms charm.

In the morning, guests gather in the dining room around a large table. Antiques and fresh flowers make this room most appealing. Nancy's fresh-baked muffins, coffee cakes, and other delicious homemade breads are served along with fresh fruit, juices, and cereal. Tea, coffee, and hot chocolate are available anytime and a late afternoon snack of Vermont cheese and crackers is offered.

The Green Mountains of southern Vermont offer abundant opportunities for outdoor enthusiasts. Dorset lies at the foot of the Green Mountains in the Mettowee Valley of rolling countryside, winding rivers, and breathtaking views. Whether your family enjoys bicycling the backroads, canoeing, hiking, or alpine skiing you are sure to find that this region offers something for you. The Merck Forest and Farmland Center is nearby and its 2800 acres offers trails and a model farm complete with work horses and hay rides. Be sure to stop at the visitor's center to see what children's activities are planned for the day. The village of Dorset and its neighboring communities are recognized for attracting some of Vermont's best auctions, craft shows, antique fairs, outdoor concerts, and renowned summer stock theatre. Nearby Manchester is a mecca for upscale outlets. The Enchanted Doll House, a museum-like collection of dolls, dollhouses, and toys, and Orvis, the fly-fishing industry's leader in outfitting anglers of all abilities, are also found in Manchester.

The Nation's first marble quarry was in Dorset. Many of the town's buildings and residences display marble in their architecture. The marble for the New York Public Library came from one of Dorset's quarries. Today the quarries, no longer in production, have become favorite swimming holes. Nancy or Allan will be happy to give you directions. Peltier's General Store in the center of the village is a great spot to put together an impromptu picnic or buy some last minute souvenirs from the selection of local Vermont products. We think you'll find this charming village and The Little Lodge at Dorset a wonderful escape anytime of year.

Accommodations: 5 guest rooms, all with private baths. Cots, crib, booster, and high chair available.

Rates: $85-$95, double occupancy, B&B. $30 for extra person in room, lower rates for children.

Methods of Payment: Cash, personal check, traveler's check preferred. American Express and Discover can be used for deposit.

Dates of Operation: Almost all year.

Children: Appropriate for all ages.

Activities/Facilities: Hiking, swimming, fishing, canoeing, golf, and tennis. Alpine and cross-country skiing nearby. Shopping, historic tours including Robert Todd Lincoln's Hildene. The Norman Rockwell Exhibition Gallery is in nearby Arlington. The Little Lodge at Dorset has a small trout pond with canoe, and a swing.

Highland Lodge

Innkeepers:David, Wilhelmina, and Alex Smith
Telephone: (802) 533-2647
Address: Caspian Lake
*   RR 1, Box 1290*
*   Greensboro, VT 05841*

The Highland Lodge is nestled amongst the rolling hills and mountains of Vermont's Northeast Kingdom on the shores of crystal clear Caspian Lake. An inexhaustible array of activities are offered at the inn year-round. The inn's private bathhouse and swimming beach along with fishing, boating, and searching for crayfish on the lake's sandy bottom will provide your family with endless hours of entertainment. Hiking trails that stretch across the inn's 120 acres and beyond, a clay tennis court, and an enormous lawn for yard games are enjoyed during the warm months of summer and the crisp days of autumn. In July and August, a supervised play program for children three to nine years old is offered at no charge. A winter wonderland unfolds as the first snowflakes fall. Highland Lodge's forty miles of cross-country trails take you through rolling fields and across frozen lakes. The Ski Touring Center at Highland Lodge offers lessons and equipment. Sledding and snowshoeing are also popular activities. For downhill enthusiasts, Stowe, Jay Peak, and Burke Mountain are all within an hour's drive.

David and Wilhelmina Smith, along with their son Alex, are wonderful hosts and have created a comfortable atmosphere for their guests. They warmly welcome families to their inn and offer personal attention to their guests' needs. Their lovely 1860 farm house boasts a large Queen Anne porch and is adorned with lush ferns and borders of perennial gardens. Four separate living rooms, each featuring a special form of entertainment and relaxation, are for lodge and cottage guests' use. A Steinway grand piano graces one of the living rooms while another houses the inn's only television. A library stocked with hundreds of classics and a good selection of magazines is a great spot to spend a quiet evening. Puzzles and games are plentiful as are comfortable sofas and rocking chairs. The inn also offers a playroom well equipped with a children's library, games, and puzzles.

There are eleven spacious and clean guest rooms in the main lodge which are appointed with country Victorian style furnishings. All rooms have private baths and can accommodate a crib or roll-away. Directly behind the lodge are ten cottages with front porches, living rooms, and woodstoves. There are one, two, and three bedroom cottages, some with kitchenettes. Four of the cottages are insulated for the winter.

Rates include both dinner and breakfast. Reasonably priced lunches are also available in the dining room Tuesday through Sunday. The kitchen will gladly pack a sack lunch for day hikes or cross-country skiing excursions. In the morning, guests partake in a full country breakfast of local farm eggs, homemade French toast smothered in maple syrup, and fresh fruit, plus many other hearty selections. In the evening, the lights are dimmed and candles are lit. Pretty pink table linens complement the dark wood furnishings. Appetizers, imaginative and delicious entrees, and sinful desserts will delight the most discriminating palates.

Whether your family is looking for a quiet getaway or an active outdoor extravaganza, the Highland Lodge is sure to be a winner.

Accommodations: 11 rooms, all with private bath in the main lodge. 10 cottages all with private baths. Cribs and roll-aways available.

Rates: $175-$215, double occupancy, MAP. Children, $20-$85, MAP. Infants 0-23 months, no charge.

Methods of Payment: Cash, traveler's check, personal check, Visa, MasterCard, and Discover.

Dates of Operation: May to October and December to March.

Children: Appropriate for all ages.

Activities/Facilities: Clay tennis court, badminton/volleyball court, horseshoes, croquet, hiking trails, swings, sandy beach, paddleboats, pulling boats, and canoes. 40 miles of cross-country ski trails, sledding, tobogganing, and snowshoeing. Cross-country ski lessons and equipment available for extra charge. Downhill skiing nearby. Many local festivities, activities, and shops.

Carolyn's Victorian Inn

Innkeeper: *Carolyn Hunter Richter*
Telephone: *(802) 472-6338, (800) 341-6338*
Address: *15 Church Street*
P.O. Box 1087
Hardwick, VT 05843

Carolyn Richter has been welcoming guests into her home since 1986. It is a beautifully maintained 100 year old Victorian with many wonderful features including original cypress woodwork, built-in cabinets and cupboards with glass doors, and high ceilings throughout. Carolyn is a gracious and accommodating host who made us feel immediately comfortable and welcome. She offers three upstairs guest rooms sharing one and a half baths. One of the rooms is actually a two room suite with one bedroom located behind the other making it a perfect space for families. The room also has a gas fireplace. Although this room shares a bath, it does have a sink in the room which is perfect for teeth brushing and face washing. Carolyn also invites young guests to check out her "Grandmother's Closet," which houses an assortment of toys and other surprises. The entire house is crisply decorated and well-appointed. Victorian wallpapers, lots of wainscoting, and beautiful window coverings adorn every room. The living room has a piano that Carolyn invites her guests to use. A beautiful and original library room offers a quiet respite for parents. But the primary gathering place is the large, comfortable dining room. Guests and local visitors linger here throughout the day. Daily newspapers, teas, and cookies are always available. The kitchen is open to guests and an extra refrigerator can be used for baby formula, picnic supplies, and cold drinks.

Three covered porches furnished with wicker furniture and rockers are located on separate sides of the house. One looks out on a small back yard area with a picnic table which is nicely secluded for younger children. Carolyn serves a formal Victorian cream tea three afternoons a week in the summertime on the expansive front porch. It is a popular attraction for her guests and local friends and neighbors.

Breakfast is a wonderful experience at Carolyn's. Her culinary acumen produces many return visitors. Fresh baked breads, muffins, and scones accompany a typical entree of egg souffle with cheese and ham or Yorkshire pudding with Vermont maple or raspberry syrup. Luscious coffee cakes, fresh seasonal fruit, and a variety of juices, coffee, and teas round out the bountiful fare. It's not unusual to see guests nibbling, sipping, and conversing around the table until noon. Carolyn will also prepare a simple but hearty dinner of homemade soup and breads topped off with a fantastic apple crisp by prior arrangement.

Numerous family oriented activities are available in the area. Ben and Jerry's Ice Cream Factory offers guided tours as does Cold Hollow Cider Mill and Cabot Creamery. Tennis, sleigh rides, and a llama farm are nearby. Sightseeing train rides and several museums are within a short drive. Carolyn's enterprising teenage daughter makes herself available for babysitting if parents desire a quiet dinner at one of the area's fine restaurants.

Carolyn's inviting hospitality and the beauty of this charming old house will make your stay pleasurable and fulfilling.

Accommodations: 3 guest rooms sharing one full and one half bath. Roll-aways, high chairs, and cribs available.

Rates: $80-$150, double occupancy, B&B. Extra persons, $25. Children under six in parent's room $10.

Methods of Payment: Cash, traveler's check, personal check preferred. Visa and MasterCard accepted.

Dates of Operation: Open all year.

Children: Appropriate for all ages.

Activities/Facilities: Backyard picnic table and basketball hoop. Museums, petting farms, fishing, skiing, tennis, golf, Caspian Lake, antiquing, and factory tours available nearby.

The Village Inn

Innkeepers: The Snyder Family
Telephone: (802) 824-6673 (800) 669-8466
Address: RR#1 Box 215
            Landgrove, VT 05148

Your family can enjoy a trip back to the friendly rural atmosphere of nineteenth century Vermont at The Village Inn. The village of Landgrove is over 150 years old and doesn't yet have
enough residents to warrant a U.S. post office. Centered around
an original farmhouse and barn dating back to 1820, the inn
today is a prime example of "Vermont continuous architecture,"
with broad dormers and ells liberally added over the years. The
inn is located on a gravel road in a wide, gentle valley surrounded by rolling hills and mountains and is at least five miles from
the nearest highway. The Snyder family has run the inn for 34
years. Three generations of Snyders work together to make your
stay a special experience.

The atmosphere at The Village Inn is casual, friendly, and rustic. Labyrinthine hallways and staircases wind through the building providing access to the eighteen guest rooms and all the public areas which include cozy alcoves, several small sitting rooms, a large dining area, and a spacious full service lounge in the former cow barn. The entire building is clean, well maintained, and furnished with comfortable, casual furniture. Laura Ashley prints and delicate antiques are foregone in favor of a practical, functional, country decor. The Snyders provide a down home style of hospitality and we felt just like part of the family. Many of the guest rooms have multiple beds and most have private baths. Each room is unique with hand made quilts, stenciling, and some even have a rocking chair. The room we stayed in was tucked above the old living room of the original house and had a double bed plus two twins and plenty of room for a roll-away or a crib. There was also a door to an adjoining room which could be unlocked to create a roomy suite.

Don has been cooking breakfast for thirty-four years and his hearty country fare is simple and fulfilling. His blueberry pancakes with Vermont maple syrup are a favorite with return guests. A variety of eggs, cereals, breads, juices, coffee, and fresh fruit, in addition to Don's J-Bar Special, are also available. Our children enjoyed the cute animal-shaped pancakes Don likes to create for all the youngsters. Dinners are available by prior reservation in the summer and fall and are included each evening in the winter season. The hearty and imaginative meals make for an enjoyable and leisurely experience. An after dinner drink in the lounge is a great way to finish your day while mingling with other guests and the Snyders.

Summertime activities are plentiful. There is a big, heated swimming pool in the back yard along with two all-weather tennis courts, a play gym, volleyball, horseshoes, and acres of lawn and meadows. Just into the woods on the hill behind the inn is an elevated paddle tennis court and a pond stocked with trout.

Loads of hiking, horseback riding, shopping, summer theatre, and family attractions are available in the nearby area. Winter guests can choose from downhill skiing at any of three nearby resorts or can strap on the cross-country skis for a tour around the property and into the neighboring National Forest. A game room with ping-pong and foosball tables, and a jacuzzi are available at the inn. Ice skaters can spend the day on the pond out back. Horse drawn sleigh rides (carriage rides in summer) are available right from the inn's front door.

The Village Inn offers comfortable, rustic accommodations and the Snyder family specializes in easy going, friendly hospitality. Your family will enjoy a stay at this get-away-from-it-all retreat.

Accommodations: 18 guest rooms, 16 with private bath. Roll-aways, cribs, high chairs, booster seats available.

Rates: Summer; $50-$85, double occupancy, B&B. Children 5 years and under, $5, over 5 years, $20. Fall/Winter; $55-$78, per person, double occupancy, MAP. Children under 5 years, $20, over 5 years, $35.

Methods of Payment: Cash, traveler's check, personal check, Visa, MasterCard.

Dates of Operation: Late May through October and mid-December through March.

Children: Appropriate for all ages.

Activities/Facilities: Swimming, tennis, sauna, game room, play gym, lounge, VCR movies, pond, paddle tennis court, sleigh rides, carriage rides, cross-country skiing, fishing, hiking available on premises. Downhill skiing, horse back riding, family attractions, shopping, sightseeing, golf, scenic and mountain bike tours available nearby.

The Wildflower Inn

Innkeepers: Jim and Mary O'Reilly
Telephone: (802) 626-8310, (800) 627-8310
Address   Darling Hill Road
*   Lyndonville, VT 05851*

Vermont's Northeast Kingdom holds a special attraction for many who have visited this beautiful corner of New England. The Wildflower Inn is a shining star in the midst of the region's scenic splendor. Jim and Mary O'Reilly are as down to earth and accommodating as any innkeepers we've met. Since purchasing this former dairy farm in 1985, they have created an idyllic escape that is well suited to families and couples. They have seven children of their own. The inn is located on a prominent ridge and overlooks beautiful valleys and distant hills in every direction. Almost every room includes a fabulous view. Grazing livestock and patchwork farmland in the surrounding area affirm that The Wildflower is truly a "country" inn.

The inn's grounds are expansive and well tended. Large, sloping lawns with tree swings, rail fences, and alluring flower gardens provide plenty of room for guests to stroll about taking in the beautiful vistas in the afternoon or the clear, starlit sky at night. Our daughter found a unique gliding cable ride strung between two old maple trees that she was consumed with. Behind the main building is a stunning, heated swimming pool and wading pool built into the hillside and overlooking an awe-inspiring valley and rolling hillsides in the distance. Next to the inn's main building is the old barn and stable area. Guests are welcome to pet the animals, or help with feeding or laying hay in stalls. The O'Reillys maintain a small menagerie of domestic animals including cows, horses, and a donkey. The elder O'Reilly children happily provided pony rides for youngsters in the corral. A pair of gigantic draft horses is also kept on hand for the frequent hay rides in summer and sleigh rides in winter.

The inn's main building is a beautifully restored Federal style house with clapboard siding and an ell. It features a large dining room with simply adorned tables and a cozy living room with a fireplace and a nice, sunken seating area. There's also a small gift shop where Wildflower mementos can be purchased. The attached Children's Room has a bumper pool table, foosball table, board games, puzzles, and a dress-up chest filled with lots of fancy clothes for children to play with. Guests can also relax in the sauna or hot tub below the playroom.

Twenty-two guest rooms are located in several buildings in addition to the main house. We stayed in the Meadows building which has more modern accommodations and features kitchenettes, multiple beds, and a spacious bath. Several family suites are available in the main house and the carriage house. Other rooms offer multiple beds for smaller families with young children.

Breakfast is delightfully hearty with wonderful homemade muffins and coffee cakes, beautifully presented fresh fruit, and a selection of daily entrees. Full course dinners are available to inn guests and the general public. A family seating hour works great for the children. A later seating is available for adults and the O'Reilly's have "a long list of mature, responsible people" available for babysitting.

Family activities at the inn and in the local area are extensive. A duck pond behind the carriage house is a good place for ice skating in winter. Burke Mountain ski area is within minutes and offers both Nordic and alpine skiing. Lots of hiking, biking, and boating opportunities are nearby. Sledding on the inn's own hills is a popular winter pastime.

The Wildflower Inn is a special place for vacationing families. The O'Reillys and their friendly staff are helpful, gracious, and magnanimous. Your family will truly enjoy a relaxing vacation in this wondrous setting.

Accommodations: 22 guest rooms, 20 with private baths. Several family suites and multiple bed rooms. Roll-aways, cribs, high chairs, and booster seats available. Handicapped accessible unit available.

Rates: $85-$145, double occupancy, B&B. Children under 5 years, free, 6 to 11 years, $8, and 12 years or older, $15. Dinner available, with reservations preferred, at an extra charge.

Methods of Payment: Cash, traveler's check, personal check preferred. Visa, American Express, Discover, and MasterCard accepted.

Dates of Operation: Open all year except April and November.

Children: Appropriate for all ages.

Activities/Facilities: Swimming, fishing, hiking, hay/sleigh rides, VCR movies, game room, ice skating, sledding, sauna, junglegym, tennis court, batting machine and cage, soccer field available on premises. Skiing, boating, horseback riding available nearby. Annual children's Nativity pageant at the inn on Christmas Eve.

Kedron Valley Inn

Innkeepers: Max and Merrily Comins
Telephone: (802) 457-1473
Address: Route 106
*   South Woodstock, VT 05071*

The Kedron Valley Inn has long been a respite for the weary traveler. It was a stagecoach stop over 150 years ago. Although many changes have been made, the inn has maintained its original allure and now reflects innkeepers Max and Merrily Comins' distinctive country tastes and gracious hospitality. The inn is nestled on fifteen acres in a valley of the Green Mountains surrounded by rolling hills and winding country roads. The idyllic town of Woodstock is just minutes away, providing guests with boutiques, restaurants, art galleries, and antique shops. A multitude of year-round activities can be found nearby. The Comins' have put together a number of seasonal packages that combine an event or activity with lodging accommodations. For those who prefer a potpourri of things to do, summer brings swimming and sunning at the inn's large spring-fed pond. A sandy

beach, floating docks and lots of lounge chairs make this a popular hang out. A lifeguard is on duty for everyone's peace of
mind. The Billings Farm, in Woodstock, provides children with a
hands on experience at a working dairy farm and museum.
Hiking, horseback riding, golf, tennis, and bicycling can also be
found nearby. Foliage season brings driving tours and good old-
fashioned country fairs. Downhill and cross-country skiing are
wintertime favorites as are sleigh rides.

Twenty-seven spacious guest rooms filled with family heirlooms
and an extensive quilt collection are found in three separate
buildings. Families and honeymooners alike will find accommodations that provide privacy, comfort, and charm. The Log
Lodge has six rooms, all suitable for families. Each room has its
own private entrance which makes running to and from the
pond convenient and parents don't have to worry about their
children getting in the way of other guests. One of the lodge
rooms has two double beds and the other five have a double
and a twin. All of the rooms have wood burning fireplaces. The
scent from the wood logs is subtly pleasing. The 1822 Tavern has
seven rooms. Our favorite was Room 24, with a wicker daybed
and television on the first floor and a queen canopy bed with
fireplace and television on the second floor loft. A special feature
of this room is the private deck. The main inn houses fourteen
guest rooms. Writing desks, rocking chairs, canopy beds, and
wide pine wood floors grace many of the rooms. For a special
getaway, reserve Room 17 well in advance. This is the inn's most
romantic room and would be perfect for a family, too. Folding
doors separate the living room from the bedroom with a queen
canopy bed and television. The living room has a fireplace, sofa
sleeper, and television. The bathroom has two sinks, two mir-
rors, and a jacuzzi.

The dining room specializes in "nouvelle Vermont" cuisine centered around local Vermont products. An extensive wine list
complements entrees like beef tournedos with brandy and

mushroom sauce, roast country duckling with blueberry sauce, and milk-fed Vermont veal with tomatoes and garlic. Parents will be glad to know that a children's menu is also available. A full country breakfast of eggs, bacon, buttermilk pancakes, and fresh muffins is served up each morning.

A traditional New England vacation experience is waiting for you and your family at the Kedron Valley Inn.

Accommodations: 27 guest rooms, all with private baths. Cribs and roll-aways available.

Rates: $57-$95, per person, double occupancy, B&B.

Methods of Payment: Cash, traveler's check, personal check, American Express, MasterCard, and Visa.

Dates of Operation: May through March. Closed in April.

Children: Appropriate for all ages.

Activities/Facilities: 1 1/2 acre spring-fed pond with two white-sand beaches. Dining room open for break fast, lunch, and dinner. Tennis, hiking, bicycling, horseback riding, surrey and sleigh rides, canoeing, fishing, shopping, downhill and cross-country skiing nearby.

Timberholm Inn

Innkeepers: Louise and Pete Hunter
Telephone: (802) 253-7603, (800) 753-7603
Address: 452 Cottage Club Road
*   Stowe, VT 05672*

Stowe is an enchanting village in Vermont's northern ski country. Tucked into one of its wooded hillsides is where you'll find the Timberholm Inn. Its Jamestown Red, weathered exterior is rustic and charming. Pretty flower boxes and red shutters liken it to a Swiss chalet. An expansive deck along the back of the inn overlooks rolling hills and valleys. The inn's great room is warm and comfortable graced by knotty pine floors and walls. A huge fieldstone fireplace and two separate sitting areas make this a cozy setting to chat with other guests or curl up with a good book. Downstairs in the gameroom you'll find shuffleboard, darts, a television, and a VCR. A microwave oven, refrigerator, and ice are also provided for guests' convenience.

Ten uniquely decorated guest rooms are spacious and comfortable with art work and antiques. Special accommodations for families include two suites with two bedrooms each and sitting areas. Another room with a queen bed, twin bed, and trundle also works well for families. Each room has its own private bath. Innkeepers Louise and Pete Hunter offer wintertime guests an Stowe Value Package (SVP). The SVP combines an economical package of lodging and alpine lift tickets. Certain holidays are excluded, so be sure to inquire. Each morning, Louise prepares and lays out a scrumptious breakfast served buffet style. The menu changes daily and includes such treats as fresh fruit, cereals and granola, muffins, coffee cake or specialty breads, yogurt, and a unique gourmet egg or French toast dish served with real butter and Vermont maple syrup. In the summer, brownies and lemonade are set out for afternoon treats and in the winter, Louise greets apres ski guests with homemade soup and hot chocolate.

Stowe's year-round calendar of festivals, events, and activities will keep your family on the go. Summer attractions and recreational opportunities include bicycling along a six mile paved recreation path, canoeing placid mountain ponds, fishing miles of streams and rivers, horseback riding, hiking the Long Trail, and attending outdoor concerts and summer theatre. The alpine slide at Spruce Peak and the gondola at Mt. Mansfield are popular for those seeking a bit more excitement. The Stowe playground, located behind the elementary school in the village, will delight the younger set. It was designed with the help of children. An abundance of wintertime activities abounds at Stowe. Downhill and cross-country skiing enthusiasts will not be disappointed. There are over 375 acres of downhill slopes and 150 kilometers of groomed Nordic trails. Ice skating, snowshoeing, sledding, and sleigh rides will round out your stay.

The memories of fun filled days will bring you back to Stowe. The warm hospitality and comfortable accommodations will bring you back to the Timberholm Inn.

Accommodations: 10 guest rooms, all with private bath. 2 family suites. Roll-aways, cribs, high chair, and booster seat available.

Rates: $70-$130, double occupancy, B&B. Extra person, $15.

Methods of Payment: Cash, traveler's check, personal check, Visa, and MasterCard.

Dates of Operation: Open all year.

Children: Appropriate for all ages.

Activities/Facilities: Gameroom and special room for ski gear and bicycles. Bicycling, hiking, horseback riding, outdoor concerts, summer theatre. Nearby fishing, canoeing, and swimming. Wintertime activities include downhill and cross-country skiing, ice skating, snow shoeing, sleigh rides, and sledding. Day trips to Ben and Jerry's Ice Cream Factory and Cold Hollow Cider Mill. Many fine restaurants and shops.

WalkAbout Creek Lodge

Innkeepers: Joni Gaines and Andrew Hutchins
Telephone: (802) 253-7354, (800) 426-6697
Address: 199 Edson Hill Road
Stowe, VT 05672

Nestled at the foot of Mount Mansfield just minutes from Stowe's amenities you'll find WalkAbout Creek Lodge. Innkeepers Joni Gaines and Andrew "Hutch" Hutchins offer Australian hospitality at their classic mountain lodge. WalkAbout is Aboriginal for a journey of discovery. Joni and Hutch invite you to discover a truly refreshing vacation experience with "Green Mountain splendor and Australian good times."

Exposed beam ceilings, a fieldstone fireplace, and log walls create a comfortable air of country charm. A floor to ceiling fieldstone fireplace dominates the main common room. Its sunken hearth area with seating cushions is a very popular socializing place in cool spring and fall evenings and during cold winter days. A sunroom with french doors opening onto the deck is also a bright and cheery place to find guests enjoying conversation. There is a separate game room with cable television on the lower level where you'll also find The Billabong Pub which is popular with the apres ski crowd. Australian beer, a cozy fire, and new friends are enjoyed here regularly.

Visitors can choose from eleven guest rooms and a two bedroom apartment with full kitchen in the main building and two four bedroom cottages with living rooms and kitchens nestled in the woods next door. Two suites can be arranged by combining guest rooms with an adjoining bath. The guest rooms are freshly updated with comforters and window coverings to create a cozy atmosphere.

Meals are served in a large dining room on the main floor which features a wall of windows overlooking a babbling brook that runs just behind the inn. Joni serves as head chef making changes to the menu to reflect the seasons. In the summer you might savor an Australian style barbecue, while winter enjoys the more traditional gourmet four course dinner. A children's menu is available, as well as a family-style dinners. Joni's culinary skills were learned while cooking on private yachts for the rich and famous. A full Aussie country breaky (otherwise known as a full Vermont country breakfast) is served each morning to get you energized for whatever your plans may be for the day.

WalkAbout Creek Lodge rests on five acres of mostly wooded land a nice distance off Stowe's main road. An outdoor swimming pool and a clay tennis court are located behind the inn and are surrounded by a large, open yard with rock outcroppings and tidy flower beds. Cross-country skiers can access over 100 miles of local trails directly from the inn's property. Fishing, hiking, biking, horseback riding, golf, and local theatre productions provide plenty of diversion for summer visitors. Wintertime guests will enjoy downhill skiing at Vermont's highest peak, Mount Mansfield, as well as ice skating, winter carnivals, and a wealth of dining choices. Hutch and Joni are accommodating hosts who enjoy their guests and promote the casual, laid back atmosphere so befitting of Stowe. Your family will enjoy a stay here.

Accommodations: 11 guest rooms, one 2 bedroom apartment, and two 4 bedroom chalet cottages. Roll-aways, cribs, high chairs available.

Rates: $40-$65, per person, double occupancy, B&B. $60-$85, per person, double occupancy, MAP. Numerous discounts for multiple day stays, special weekends, and large groups. Inquire for extra person and children's rates.

Methods of Payment: Cash, traveler's check, personal check, Visa, MasterCard.

Dates of Operation: Open all year.

Children: Appropriate for all ages.

Activities/Facilities: Swimming, hiking, tennis, lawn games available on premises. Alpine and Nordic skiing, horseback riding, summer theatre, fishing, and plentiful family attractions in the area.

The Lareau Farm Country Inn

Innkeepers: Susan and Dan Easley
Telephone: (802) 496-4949, (800) 833-0766
Address: Box 563
*   Route 100*
*   Waitsfield, VT 05673*

The Lareau Farm Country Inn is perfect for a family country get-away. Nestled along the Mad River in a pastoral, mountain rimmed valley, the inn offers lots of country style activities and clean, comfortable lodging. Susan and Dan Easley provide a welcoming hospitality that has earned the inn recognition as one of the "Top 50 Inns in America" in a guest survey conducted by Inn Times magazine. White clapboard siding, a wide front porch, a red barn, and white fences welcome arriving visitors. Parts of the building date to the late 1700's, but it was mostly constructed in 1832 by Simeon Stoddard, Waitsfield's first physician. The Easleys have done a wonderful job of remodeling and adding some additional guest rooms. Two first floor living rooms, one with a TV and one with a fireplace, offer quaint places for mingling or enjoying an evening movie. But the main floor is dominated by a beautiful, large dining room with simply decorated tables, and a bay of panoramic windows overlooking meadows, woods, and the river. A fireplace adds warmth in the winter and guests gather over afternoon apres ski snacks. The dining room opens to a large wraparound covered porch which is a great place for parents to relax while the kids romp in the yard. The inn also offers a unique factory tour to guests. American Flatbreads operates a small bakery at the inn. Their pizza-like bread is baked in a wood fired earthen oven and is a flavorful treat for many inn guests. Children enjoy watching the dough preparation and baking process and the end result can serve as a good family lunch.

Thirteen roomy and tastefully restored guest rooms are available. Susan made the country quilts gracing each bed. In the old section of the house, some nice work has been done to expose and remodel around original beams and framing. Charming wallpaper, stenciled walls, and antique brass or hardwood beds are featured in every room. Several rooms provide multiple beds, one with a double and two singles.

Dan provides horse drawn sleigh rides on the inn's sixty-seven acres in the winter. Their seven horses, Holly, Dolly, Molly, Polly, Don, Ben, and Gerrie tour the meadow daily with full loads of bundled guests. Four dogs and four cats make up what is commonly known as the "Lareau Zoo." Cross-country skiing is also available on the property and on hundreds of miles of groomed trails in the valley. Downhill skiing at Sugarbush and Mad River Glen is minutes away. Summertime activities include hiking, biking, canoeing, fishing, and swimming in a clear, shallow Mad River swimming hole. There is also plenty of antique shopping and sightseeing in the area. Dan and Susan will show you where to picnic in the meadow or down by the river. Full country breakfasts will get your day started right. Fresh seasonal fruit, poached pears, or baked apples are accompanied by farm fresh eggs, bacon, and pancakes. Susan uses ingredients from the inn's garden or neighboring farms as much as possible. The hearty fare is aromatic and fulfilling. Dinners can be arranged for groups or special evenings. Lareau Farm participates in seasonal inn-to-inn progressive dinners and offers a very special Thanksgiving package including four nights lodging, breakfasts, a full Thanksgiving turkey dinner, and several other meals. It's a popular annual event.

The Easleys' friendly, easygoing style and the beautiful facilities they offer will likely make your family another of their many return visitors.

Accommodations: 13 rooms, 11 with private baths. Several rooms with multiple beds.

Rates: $60-$100, double occupancy, B&B. $10-$20 for extra persons in the room. Midweek discounts, extended stay rates, and package plans available.

Methods of Payment: Cash, traveler's check, personal check preferred. Visa and MasterCard accepted.

Dates of Operation: Open all year.

Children: Appropriate for all ages.

Activities/Facilities: Swimming, fishing, hiking, sleigh rides, games, puzzles, cross-country skiing available on premises. Downhill skiing, soaring, canoeing, shopping, sightseeing, fine dining in the vicinity.

The Mad River Inn

Innkeepers: Rita and Luc Maranda
Telephone: (802) 496-7900 (800) 832-8278
Address: P.O. Box 75
*   Waitsfield, VT 05673*

Rita and Luc Maranda opened The Mad River Inn Bed and Breakfast in 1989. They thought this large, old Victorian farmhouse nestled on seven acres of riverside meadows and woods would make a wonderful traditional bed and breakfast establishment. After some necessary remodeling and a beautiful job of interior decoration, their hopes have been realized. The Mad River Inn is a beautiful home base from which to explore the many splendors of Vermont's scenic Mad River Valley. Rita and Luc offer a youthful and enthusiastic brand of hospitality and are occasionally assisted by their seven year old son, Jessee.

The inn offers an elegant ambiance while maintaining a comfortable, family friendly feel. On the main floor, a beautifully decorated parlor room with rich, flowing draperies and floral print

Victorian furnishings welcomes guests returning from their day's activities. The adjoining dining room is also a comfortable, well appointed gathering place. A great area for children is the downstairs playroom which is stocked with toys, games, and books. There is also a lounge area with a television, a wood-stove, billiards, and a small B.Y.O.B bar. The entire basement is furnished with contemporary couches and chairs and is very comfortable for families. Ten guest rooms are located on the second floor and each is decorated with its own color theme and gorgeous brass, wicker, or hardwood antique beds. European featherbeds are used in every room. If you have never slept on a featherbed, you're in for a treat. Rita and Luc have a wonderful sense of decor and all the guest rooms are immediately warm and inviting. Lots of windows, bright, fluffy bed linens, lots of flowers, and neatly displayed collectibles create a comfortable and relaxing environment guaranteed to provide a good night's sleep. Most rooms are large enough for a crib or roll-away. Several suite arrangements can be made by combining adjoining rooms.

A full country breakfast greets guests each morning. The Marandas possess culinary skills that rival their decorating acumen. A parade of fresh squeezed juices, coffees, muffins, and fruits accompany a daily entree of eggs or griddle cakes with Vermont maple syrup. Full course gourmet dinners are available for groups by prior arrangement. Many of the seasonal herbs, fruits, and vegetables used in guests meals are grown in Rita and Luc's own organic garden. Children are welcome to explore the garden and sample the bounty. In autumn, your kids will enjoy choosing a nice big pumpkin to take home.

The grounds at the Mad River Inn are spacious and open. A large back yard is framed by pastoral views of the Mad River Valley and surrounding hillsides. At the edge of the lawn is a pretty gazebo, perfect for afternoon lemonade in the summer. Guests can also use the gas barbecue grill for picnic dinners if they choose. There is also a large hammock for old-fashioned country naps.

Plenty of activities are available in the Waitsfield area. Ice skating on the inn's pond, sleigh rides, snowmobiling, and plenty of Nordic and alpine skiing are available in winter months. Mad River canoeing, swimming, fishing, bicycling, horseback riding, and seasonal festivals will keep you busy the rest of the year. The Mad River Inn offers a uniquely elegant yet comfortable getaway your family is sure to enjoy.

Accommodations: 10 guest rooms, all with private baths. Rollaways, cribs, high chairs available. French spoken.

Rates: $75-$150, double occupancy, B&B. $20 per additional person. Children 2 years and under, free.

Methods of Payment: Cash, traveler's check, personal check preferred. Visa, MasterCard, American Express accepted.

Dates of Operation: Open all year.

Children: Appropriate for all ages.

Activities/Facilities: Afternoon tea and treats, children's playroom, yard games, fishing, ice skating, billiards, jacuzzi, and barbecue equipment available on premises. Downhill and Nordic skiing, shopping, hiking, bicycling, horseback and sleigh rides, golf, snowmobiling, scenic drives, family attractions available nearby.

Deer Brook Inn

Innkeepers: Brian and Rosemary McGinty
Telephone: (802) 672-3713
Address: HCR 68, Box 443
             Route 4
             Woodstock, VT 05091

The Deer Brook Inn is located along a rather solitary stretch of road between some of Vermont's most popular destinations. Just eight miles to the east of Killington ski resort and four miles to the west of historic Woodstock Village, it affords guests a relaxed respite from bustling crowds. This is a small inn, with only four guest rooms, so your stay will be personal and intimate. Brian and Rosemary McGinty are easygoing and warm, and their gracious hospitality will make you feel right at home. The McGintys have two young children, James and Kelly and a mother-daughter pair of Golden Retrievers named Sage and Nutmeg. Both dogs are mellow and friendly. Sage loves to play fetch with visiting children.

When they first purchased the property, Brian and Rosemary undertook a complete gutting and reconstruction of the house's interior. They retained the original wide pine flooring, many of the fixtures and cabinets, and much of the original wood trim-work. Beyond that, everything on the inside of the Deer Brook Inn is new and modern. Rosemary has done extensive stenciling on the walls throughout the house. She has also handmade quilts for all the beds. The main floor features a well appointed living room with magazines and books and a TV for evening relaxing. Numerous paintings and drawings by local artists are displayed on the walls and are for sale. Behind the living room is a large dining room with a table that could seat as many as twelve. A wall of double hung windows on one side of the room provides lots of natural light and peaceful views of the meadow out back. One of the windows has been modified with one way glass to produce a feeding aviary for cardinals, finches, and other local birds. Our children loved watching the endless parade of hungry visitors.

The four guest rooms are all located upstairs, one on each corner of the house, and each has a private bath. All rooms have queen or king-size beds. They are simply and comfortably decorated with antique beds and furnishings, and the aforementioned pine floors and stenciled walls. There is plenty of room for a roll-away or a crib. The bathrooms are spacious, clean, and modern.

Rosemary's breakfasts are hearty, creative, and nicely presented. The aromas emanating from her kitchen will roust you from a good night's rest in the country air. Fresh seasonal fruits and a variety of home baked muffins served with coffee and juices begin your meal. We particularly enjoyed her banana walnut chocolate chip muffins. A main course follows, featuring omelets or French toast, with bacon, sausage, or ham. After a second cup of coffee and some friendly conversation, Rosemary will gladly point you toward your preference of popular or lesser known activities abundant in the area.

Vermont

Brian and Rosemary McGinty have created a peaceful haven in the heart of the Vermont countryside. Your family will surely enjoy this quaint, comfortable getaway.

Accommodations: 4 rooms with private baths. Roll-aways, cribs, high chairs, and booster seats available.

Rates: $65-$85, double occupancy, B&B.

Methods of Payment: Cash, traveler's check, personal check, MasterCard, Visa.

Dates of Operation: Open all year.

Children: Appropriate for all ages.

Activities/Facilities: Downhill and cross-country skiing, golf, hiking, swimming, fishing, shopping, fine dining, sightseeing available in the area.

Index